Go and Have a Good Time

Learning Activities for School-Time Vacations

by Rose West

To Arcadia School Media Center.
I hope you use & enjoy this book

Rose West

Fearon Teacher Aids
Simon & Schuster Supplementary Education Group

This book is dedicated with love to my daughter,
Dr. Sue West Phillips, and to my parents,
Hulda and Tony Timmerman

Acknowledgments

I would like to acknowledge the following people for their help and support in putting this book together:

Thomas Fitch, Ph.D., project
  director of the Honors Project
  for Outstanding Teachers of
  Science in the State of Illinois,
  1984–1988
Donna Bell
Melissa Bonebrake
Paul Caulfield
Kelly Feeney
Earnestine Foster
Jennifer Grogg
Laura Marksteiner

Melissa Marozik
Marilyn Morey
Judy Paske
Lee Pensinger
Dr. Jeffrey Phillips
Robin Sanderson
Todd Stelter
Julia Townsend
Linda C. Vance
Bill West

and all of the teachers of the Illinois Honors Project: Charles Baum, Tony Brieler, Albertine Burget, Bob Burtch, Bill Conrad, Gloria Dobry, Marilyn Donalson, Marlisa Ebeling, John Figlewicz, Tom Graika, Marlene Gregor, Keith Hanson, Maureen Jamrock, Barbara Janes, Yvonne Johnson, Mary Kelly, Doug Kuban, Chris Linas, Linda Morris, Don Nelson, Barb Quickstad, Larry Reinhard, Trish Roderick, Joe Sidwell, Marilyn Sinclair, Fred Tarnow, Sharon Travous, Carl Van DeWalle, Edee Wiziecki, and Marilyn Zito.

Illustrated and designed by Rose Sheifer

ISBN 0-8224-3500-4

Printed in the United States of America
1. 9 8 7 6 5 4 3 2 1

CONTENTS

INTRODUCTION

"Go and have a good time" is what many teachers say to a student who is going to miss school because of a family vacation. Other teachers, in contrast, load the student with so much makeup work that he or she cannot enjoy the trip. This book offers an alternative to those two responses—activities that enable the student not only to "go and have a good time" but also to become more aware of the places he or she visits and to learn during the trip.

The activities in this book are designed to be used when vacations will take students out of school. *They are meant to take the place of regular school work, not to be additional tasks.* Most of the activities are science-related, but some involve social studies or math, and others exercise writing or communications skills.

Standard Assignments and Special Activities

Every vacationing student should do two standard assignments: keep a log book (see "Log Book Instructions," page 20) and record travel data (see "Travel Data," pages 22–26). Keeping track of travel data (such as miles traveled each day and the number of miles per gallon of fuel) calls on math skills. Keeping the log book requires a variety of language arts skills. This assignment requires the student not only to record daily sights and events but also to interview two people—one along the way and one at the vacation spot. Because the student must also include a map on which he or she labels the places visited and traces the travel route, the log book provides a geography lesson, too. And even though the primary purpose of the log book is to give the student practice with a variety of academic skills, it will also be a lasting memento of a special trip.

The rest of the reproducible activity pages outline projects that will stimulate learning experiences at a variety of vacation sites—from amusement parks to zoos. The students use their log books to record most of the projects (except for the arts and crafts activities). The information to be recorded in the log book is indicated by the symbol ✏. The number and kinds of activities you assign will depend on the student, the vacation site, and the length of the trip.

After the student returns from the trip, he or she will probably be eager to share the adventure with classmates. Allot some time for the student to show slides, photographs, or drawings and tell about interesting experiences during the trip. If your student has collected a number of "treasures," he or she might want to make a display box for them (see "How to Make a Display Box," page 27).

Vacation Contract and Evaluation

It is a good idea for each vacationing student to sign a contract (in triplicate) to indicate that he or she understands the requirements and agrees to do the tasks. (See "Vacation Assignment Contract," page 19.) Keep one copy of the contract, and give one copy to the student and one to the parent or adult going on the trip.

The method of evaluation should be a part of the contract so that the student knows what is expected of him or her. To evaluate the log book and the activities, you might give a certain number of points for each area—for example, ten points for the map, five for neatness, and so on. The other activities can be graded with the log or treated separately. Middle school and junior high school teachers might want to evaluate the parts of the log book and the activities by subject area. Whatever method you choose for evaluation, set your standards—taking the student's age and ability into consideration—before evaluating the materials.

Other Ways to Use These Activities

Some students never go on a vacation during school time and travel only during the regular winter, spring, and summer vacations. For them, assign the log book and appropriate activities as extra credit.

Other students rarely take a vacation outside their hometown. These students could keep log books and do appropriate activities in their own backyards or nearby parks. For example, in the winter students in northern states could do "Snowdrift Adventure" (page 74) and "Snowflake Observation" (page 75). Students anywhere at almost any time of the year could do any of the nature-observation activities—from "Bird Watching" (page 33) to "Stargazing" (page 79).

Many of these activities for trips to various kinds of museums and other institutions can also be used on class field trips.

STATE TOURISM BUREAUS

Tourism bureaus will provide valuable information about their state free of charge. In preparation for their vacations and the activities they plan to do, students might write to the state (or states) they plan to visit. Or as part of a language arts assignment, the teacher could have all students write to different states at the beginning of the school year. This information could be kept in the room resource area for use by all students when needed.

Alabama: Bureau of Tourism and Travel, 532 S. Perry Street, Montgomery, AL 36104

Alaska: Alaska Division of Tourism, P.O. Box E, Juneau, AK 99811-0800

Arizona: Arizona Office of Tourism, 1480 E. Bethany Home Road, Suite 180, Phoenix, AZ 85014

Arkansas: Arkansas Department of Parks and Tourism, One Capitol Mall, Little Rock, AR 72201

California: California Office of Tourism, Department of Commerce, 1121 L Street, Suite 600, Sacramento, CA 95814

Colorado: Colorado Tourism Board, 1625 Broadway, Suite 1700, Denver, CO 80202

Connecticut: Tourism Promotion Service, State Department of Economic Development, 210 Washington Street, Hartford, CT 06106

Delaware: Delaware Tourism Office, 99 Kings Highway, P.O. Box 1401, Dover, DE 19903

Florida: Department of Commerce, Visitors Inquiry, 126 Van Buren Street, Tallahassee, FL 32399-2000

Georgia: Tourist Division, P.O. Box 1776, Atlanta, GA 30301

Hawaii: Department of Business and Economic Development, P.O. Box 2359, Honolulu, HI 96804

Idaho: Idaho Travel Council Administrative Office, Idaho Department of Commerce, State Capitol Building, Boise, ID 83720

Illinois: Illinois Office of Tourism, 310 South Michigan Avenue, Suite 108, Chicago, IL 60604

Indiana: Indiana Department of Commerce, Tourism Division, 1 North Capitol, Suite 700, Indianapolis, IN 46204

Iowa: Bureau of Tourism and Visitors, Iowa Department of Economic Development, 200 E. Grand Avenue, Des Moines, IA 50309

Kansas: Kansas Department of Commerce, Travel and Tourism Division, 400 W. 8th Street, 5th Floor, Topeka, KS 66603-3957

Kentucky: Kentucky Department of Travel Development, Capital Plaza Tower, Frankfort, KY 40601

Louisiana: Louisiana Office of Tourism, P.O. Box 94291, Baton Rouge, LA 70804-9291

Maine: Maine Tourism Information Services, Maine Publicity Bureau, 97 Winthrop Street, P.O. Box 2300, Hallowell, ME 04347-2300

Maryland: Office of Tourist Development, 45 Calvert Street, Annapolis, MD 21401

Massachusetts: Massachusetts Office of Travel and Tourism, 100 Cambridge Street, 13th Floor, Boston, MA 02202

Michigan: Travel Bureau, Michigan Department of Commerce, P.O. Box 30226, Lansing, MI 48909

Minnesota: Minnesota Office of Tourism, 375 Jackson Street, 250 Skyway Level, St. Paul, MN 55101-1810

Mississippi: Mississippi Department of Economic Development, Division of Tourism, P.O. Box 849, Jackson, MS 39205-0849

Missouri: Highway and Transportation Department, P.O. Box 270, Jefferson City, MO 05102

Montana: Travel Montana, Department of Commerce, 1424 9th Avenue, Helena, MT 59620

Nebraska: Department of Economic Development, Division of Travel and Tourism, P.O. Box 94666, Lincoln, NE 68509

Nevada: Commission of Tourism, Capitol Complex, Carson City, NV 89710

New Hampshire: New Hampshire Office of Vacation Travel, P.O. Box 856, Concord, NH 03301

New Jersey: Division of Travel and Tourism, Department of Commerce, Energy, and Economic Development, CN-826, Trenton, NJ 08625

New Mexico: Economic Development and Tourism Department, Tourism and Travel Division, Joseph Montoya Building, 1100 St. Francis Drive, Santa Fe, NM 87502

New York: State of New York Department of Commerce, Division of Tourism, One Commerce Plaza, Albany, NY 12245

North Carolina: North Carolina Division of Travel and Tourism, Department of Commerce, 430 N. Salisbury Street, Raleigh, NC 27603

North Dakota: North Dakota Tourism Promotion, Liberty Memorial Building, State Capitol Grounds, Bismarck, ND 58505

Ohio: Ohio Division of Travel and Tourism, P.O. Box 1001, Columbus, OH 43266-0101

Oklahoma: Oklahoma Tourism and Recreation Department, 500 Will Rogers Building, Oklahoma City, OK 73105

Oregon: Tourism Division, Oregon Economic Development Department, 595 Cottage Street, NE, Salem, OR 97310

Pennsylvania: Department of Tourism Promotions, 416 Forum Building, Harrisburg, PA 17101

Rhode Island: Bureau of Tourism of Rhode Island, 7 Jackson Walkway, Providence, RI 02903

South Carolina: South Carolina Division of Tourism, Suite 110, Edgar A. Brown Building, 1205 Pendleton Street, Columbia, SC 29201

South Dakota: Department of Tourism, Capital Lake Place, 711 Wells, Pierre, SD 57501

Tennessee: Tennessee Department of Tourist Development, P.O. Box 23170, Nashville, TN 37202

Texas: Travel and Information Division, P.O. Box 5064, Austin, TX 78763-5064

Utah: Utah Travel Council, Council Hall, Capitol Hill, Salt Lake City, UT 84114

Vermont: Vermont Travel Division, 134 State Street, Montpelier, VT 05602

Virginia: Virginia Division of Tourism, 202 N. Ninth Street, Suite 500, Richmond, VA 23219

Washington: State of Washington Department of Trade and Economic Development, 101 General Administration Building, AX-13, Olympia, WA 98504-0013

West Virginia: Department of Commerce, State Capitol Complex, Charleston, WV 25305

Wisconsin: Wisconsin Division of Tourism Development, P.O. Box 7670, Madison, WI 53707

Wyoming: Wyoming Travel Commission, Frank Norris Jr. Travel Center, Cheyenne, WY 82002-0660

ACTIVITY KEY

Arts and Crafts	Language Arts	Math	Science	Social Studies	Amusement Parks & Outdoor Exhibitions	Camping Trips	Car Travel	Mountains and Lakes	Museums & Indoor Exhibitions	Nature Observation	Seashore and Ocean	Stay-at-Home Projects	Urban Vacations	Winter Activities	Activity
			X		X										Amusement Park Visit: Centripetal Force
			X		X										Amusement Park Visit: The Coriolis Force
			X		X										Amusement Park Visit: Pulse Rate
	X		X						X	X			X		Aquarium Visit
	X		X							X	X				Beach Exploration
			X					X	X	X	X	X			Bird Watching
	X		X							X					Cave Exploration
X	X	X	X	X								X			Cemetery Exploration
	X			X								X			City, Town, or Village Excursion
		X	X				X								Color in Your World
		X	X							X		X		X	Color My World with Snow
				X								X			Factory Visit
		X	X							X					Farm Visit
		X	X					X		X	X				Fishing Trip
		X	X									X			Geology Comparison
X			X			X				X	X				Hammered Leaf and Flower Prints
	X		X				X			X					Lake Exploration
X			X			X				X	X				Making Dyes
			X							X	X			X	Metamorphosis of Snow
	X	X	X			X	X			X					Mountain Excursion
	X	X					X					X			Music, Music, Music
	X		X							X					National Park Excursion
	X		X						X			X			Natural History Museum Visit: Dinosaurs
			X						X			X			Natural History Museum Visit: Habitat Scene
		X		X					X			X			Natural History Museum Visit: Indians
	X			X					X			X			Natural History Museum Visit: Mummies
X	X		X			X				X	X				Painted Leaf Prints
			X							X					Park, Forest Preserve, or Nature Center Visit
			X					X		X			X		Planetarium Visit
			X									X			The Playground: Swing Science
			X			X				X		X			Rock Classification I and II
	X		X					X					X		Science Museum Visit
X	X		X		X					X			X		Sea Life Park Visit
X		X								X		X			Seed Pictures
X			X							X		X			Shadow Pictures
			X							X	X				Shell Collection I and II
	X		X											X	Skiing: Pulse Rate
		X	X							X		X		X	Snowdrift Adventure
X		X	X					X		X		X		X	Snowflake Observation
	X		X										X		Space Center Visit
			X			X				X		X			Stargazing
X			X			X				X		X			Sun Prints
			X							X	X				Tidepools
X	X	X	X			X				X		X			Trees
	X			X									X		Washington, D.C., Visit
		X	X							X			X		Weather Comparison
	X		X			X				X					Wild Flowers
X			X			X				X					Wild Foods
	X								X			X			Write a Poem
			X		X					X			X		Zoo Excursion: Birds & Mammals & Reptiles

ANSWER KEY AND ACTIVITY INSTRUCTIONS

Amusement Park Visit: Centripetal Force, page 28

1. The sinker stays in the same place whether the bottle is upside down or right-side up.
2. The force of the spinning (or the tension) keeps the sinker in the same place.
3. *(The diagram could show the bottle in different positions with the sinker always in the middle of the bottle.)*
4. *Answers will vary.*
5. When you whirl a stone around on a string, you must hold the string tight to keep the stone from flying off in a straight line. The force the string applies to the object is the centripetal force.

Amusement Park Visit: The Coriolis Force, page 29

1. The nerf balls seem to curve. (But they really go straight.)
2. The rotation of the ride causes this to happen. The ride spins while the ball goes straight.
3. When a spaceship goes up, it won't come down in the same place, because the earth rotates. The earth's rotation has to be taken into account to determine where the ship will land.

Cave Exploration, page 34

7. When water drips through cracks in the roof of the cave, it carries the mineral calcite with it. Stalactites and stalagmites are formed as the water evaporates and leaves the calcite.
8. Stalactites and stalagmites are still getting larger if water is continuing to seep into the cave.
9. Different minerals and chemicals mixed with the calcite (which is the major ingredient of limestone) create the different colors in the stalactites and stalagmites.

Cemetery Exploration, page 35
This activity has many aspects—science, social studies, math, language arts, and art. The student may do all the parts or only certain ones.

Color in Your World, page 40
Use Color Wheel I for primary grade students. Use Color Wheel II for upper elementary and middle school students.

Hammered Leaf and Flower Prints, page 48
Remind the student, if he or she is going to be flying to the vacation site, not to take the hammer along in carry-on luggage!

Mountain Excursion, page 52

1. Young mountains have sharper peaks than the older mountains have. Older mountains have been worn away due to erosion and weathering. For example, the Rocky Mountains are young mountains, and the Appalachian Mountains are older mountains.

Natural History Museum Visits, pages 57–60
Although natural history museums include a wide variety of exhibits, only four kinds of exhibits have been selected here. If the student is interested in another topic, you might help him or her to adapt one of these activity sheets for that topic.

Natural History Museum Visit: Mummies, page 60

9. Ancient Egyptians placed their dead in tombs. Some people today are buried in tombs. The ancient Egyptians also buried treasures with their loved ones. People who are buried in tombs today might also have special objects buried with them.
10. Servants and objects needed in life were buried with the mummy for the voyage to the underworld or for life after death.

Planetarium Visit, page 63
PLANETS

4.

PLANET	DIAMETER (miles)	MOONS	DISTANCE FROM SUN (million miles)
Mercury	3,100	0	36
Venus	7,500	0	67
Earth	7,900	1	93
Mars	4,200	2	142
Jupiter	89,400	16	484
Saturn	74,980	17	887
Uranus	32,490	5	1,783
Neptune	30,760	2	2,794
Pluto	1,500 (est.)	1	3,670

GALAXIES

5. Spiral galaxies (which are disc shaped with a bulge at the center and with arms spiraling out like a pinwheel), elliptical galaxies (which are oval shaped and have no spiral arms), and irregular galaxies (which are irregularly shaped).

6. Our solar system is in the Milky Way, which is a spiral galaxy.

7. The nearest galaxies to the Milky Way are the Large and Small Magellanic Clouds, which were named after explorer Ferdinand Magellan. They are about 170,000 light years away and are satellite galaxies of the Milky Way.

8. *Answers may include* the Andromeda Nebula, which can be seen only from the Northern Hemisphere and is about 2 million light years away, and Cygnus A, which is about 500 million light years away and can be detected only by radio telescope.

CONSTELLATIONS

9. *Answers will vary.*

10. Astronomers in ancient Egypt and Greece divided the sky into constellations, or areas that had fairly distinct groups of stars. If imaginary lines were drawn between the stars in each group or in an outline around them, representations of figures could be created. The ancient astronomers named these groups of stars after mythological heroes, heroines, and animals. Most of the names we use for constellations today are those devised by the ancient Greeks.
Answers about specific constellations will vary.

TELESCOPES

11. The *refracting telescope* uses a lens to collect light. The light forms an image, which is magnified. The *reflecting telescope* uses a curved mirror to gather light. It also uses a lens to magnify the image. These two telescopes are optical telescopes. The *radio telescope* is used to collect radio waves from objects in space. It has a huge saucer-shaped reflector that collects electromagnetic waves. These waves are then focused on other antennas that feed the waves as electrical impulses into radio receivers. The impulses are reproduced as wavy lines on paper.

12. The first refracting telescope was invented by a Dutch optician, Hans Lippershey, in 1608. The Italian astronomer Galileo built a telescope in 1609 after hearing about Lippershey's invention. With his telescope, Galileo discovered the rings of Saturn, four of Jupiter's moons, and mountains and craters on the earth's moon.

Sir Isaac Newton built one of the first reflecting telescopes. It is known as the Newtonian telescope. Another type of reflecting telescope was invented by N. Cassegrain of France. It is known as the Cassegrainian telescope.

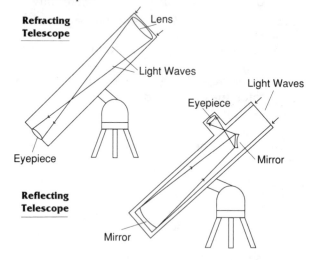

The radio telescope was developed after World War II. An American engineer, Karl Jansky, first identified radio waves from space in 1931.

13. The largest reflecting telescope in the world is on Mt. Pastukhov in the Soviet Union. The mirror is over 236 inches (600 cm) in diameter. The largest reflecting telescope in the United States is at Mount Palomar Observatory in California. The mirror is 200 inches (508 cm) in diameter.

14. The largest refracting telescope in the world is at Yerkes Observatory in Williams Bay, Wisconsin. The objective lens has a diameter of 40 inches (102 cm). The tube is 63 feet (19 m) long.

Extra Credit Question: In 1989 the space shuttle *Discovery* was scheduled to carry into orbit the Edwin P. Hubble Space Telescope. This is a 12-ton (the size of a bus) space-based observatory. The Hubble Space Telescope is the most precise telescope ever built. It will see ten times farther into deep space than ground-based telescopes can and will not be hindered by the earth's atmosphere. The telescope has a 94.5-inch primary mirror and a lens that weighs 2,000 pounds.

The Playground: Swing Science, page 64

1. *The variables might include* the weight of the person swinging, the height of the person pulling the swing back, the length of the chains of the swing, the length of the arc of each swing, and the amount of friction on the chain's pivot point.

2. *The conditions for the greatest number of swings might include* a swing with short chains, a light person swinging, a short person pulling the swing back.

Rock Classification, pages 65 and 66

Use Rock Classification I for primary grade students. Use Rock Classification II for upper elementary and middle school students.

Shell Collection, pages 71 and 72

Use Shell Collection I for primary grade students. Use Shell Collection II for upper elementary and middle school students.

Snowdrift Adventure, page 74

1. The level of the snowdrift that is coldest depends on the outside air temperature. Usually, the innermost level will be warmest, and the outside layers will be colder.

2. The air can get colder than snow, because ice can be only 32°F.

3. The innermost layer will probably be the thickest because the snow in each subsequent layer has to spread out farther to cover the mound of snow underneath it.

Space Center Visit, page 78

1. Unmanned satellites are classified according to their purpose. The six main types of satellites are (1) weather satellites, used to collect data for long-range weather forecasts; (2) earth observation satellites, used to collect data about the earth (there are two types: geodetic satellites, which collect information about the shape, gravitational field, and topography of the earth, and earth resource satellites, which collect data about the oceans, the earth's crust, pollution, and the location of natural resources); (3) communication satellites, used to relay radio, television, and teletype messages; (4) applications technology satellites (ATS), used to test new equipment in space; (5) biosatellites, used to test the effects of weightlessness, cosmic and solar radiation, acceleration, and other effects of space on biological specimens; (6) physics and astronomy satellites, used to collect data about the sun, the earth's atmosphere, space, and the galaxies.

2. *Answers might include the following:*

   - Project Mercury (1958–1963) was the first manned project in the program to send people to the moon. It carried one astronaut for a short period of time. Its goals were to test people's ability to survive in space, to develop hardware for later space flights, to test spacecraft re-entry systems, and to establish an around-the-world tracking system.

   - Project Gemini (1964–1966) was the second phase in the program to send people to the moon. The craft was designed to carry two astronauts for two weeks or more. Its goals were to test two astronauts and equipment during a long flight, to rendezvous and dock with other orbiting vehicles, to maneuver the docked vehicles in space, and to gain more information about the effects of space on the physical conditions of the crew.

   - Project Apollo (1966–1972) was the final stage in the program to send people to the moon. The spacecraft was designed for three astronauts and was much larger than previous spacecrafts. Its goals were to land U.S. astronauts on the moon, to place scientific stations on the moon's surface, to develop technology for advanced space exploration, and to return the astronauts safely to earth.

   - Skylab (1973) was an experimental space station program designed to expand knowledge of space and manned earth-orbital operations. A three-person crew worked on the space station. The Skylab included the Orbital Workshop, the Apollo Telescope Mount, the Airlock Module, and the Multiple Docking Adapter. Its goals were to study earth-sun interrelationships and other space phenomena; to gather data for use in oceanography, water management, agriculture, forestry, geology, and ecology; to determine the effects of long-duration space flights on people and space vehicles; and to find ways in which the space environment could be utilized in developing new materials or new forms of known materials.

   - The Apollo-Soyuz Test Project (1975) was a joint project of the United States and the Soviet Union. Its goal was to test the compatibility of systems for docking future manned spacecraft of the U.S. and the USSR.

- The Space Shuttle (1981–present) is a space exploration system designed to carry out various missions in earth orbit. The shuttle and rocket boosters are designed to be reused. Its goals have been to perfect a spacecraft that can be launched with rocket boosters, stay in earth orbit up to 30 days, and return to earth by landing like an airplane; to carry out various experiments in a weightless environment; and to use personnel who are not fully trained astronauts to carry out scientific and technical duties.

3. *Many experiments have been performed on space shuttle flights. The following are a sampling of them. Student answers may include others.*
   - The Effect of Weightlessness on Bees. The purpose of this experiment was to determine whether bees can adapt to weightlessness. It was learned that bees could adapt to weightlessness. The bees in space built a honeycomb similar to the honeycomb a control group built on the ground.
   - Chicken Embryo Development in Space. Thirty-two fertile eggs were placed in a box and put on *Discovery,* and another 32 fertile eggs were kept on earth. The purpose was to determine whether any changes in the developing embryo could be attributed to microgravity.
   - The Effects of Weightlessness on the Healing Bone. The purpose of this experiment was to establish whether the environmental effects of space flight inhibit bone healing.
   - Utilizing a Semipermeable Membrane to Direct Crystal Growth. The purpose of this experiment was to produce purer and larger lead crystals that may help improve X-ray film resolution.
   - The Effects of Weightlessness on Grain Formation and Strength in Metals. The purpose of this experiment was to investigate the formation of titanium grain in microgravity.

4. All rocks on the moon are igneous rocks formed by the cooling of molten lava. No sedimentary or metamorphic rocks are found on the moon. The dark regions of the moon are basalt. The light regions are older

and made of the rocks gabbro, norite, and anorthosite. The Apollo 15 crew brought back samples of lunar lava that were judged to be 3 billion years old. The Apollo 17 crew brought back a rock called troctolite, which is made of the minerals olivine and feldspar. It is 4.6 billion years old and may have been some of the first material to solidify when the moon was formed. Moon rock is quite different from earth rock because there is no water on the moon or in the rocks. Samples of moon rock were also returned by Apollos 11, 12, 14, and 16.

5. A spacesuit such as one worn on the moon requires the following items not found on average clothing: helmet, protective visor, oxygen hoses, protective garment, portable life-support system, lunar boots, and other equipment used for collecting samples or taking pictures.

   Shuttle suits are simpler. They are pressure suits like those worn by military jet pilots. They are worn only during launch and re-entry; when the shuttle is in orbit, the crew members wear regular clothing. The shuttle suit includes an upper and a lower torso that snap together with seal rings. A life-support system is built into the upper torso.

6. *A basic time line of the space program would include the following entries:*

1958–1963	Project Mercury
1964–1966	Project Gemini
1966–1972	Project Apollo
1972	Pioneer 10 (space probe)
1973	Skylab
1975	Apollo-Soyuz Test Project
1977	Voyagers 1 and 2 (space probes)
1981	Columbia (first space shuttle)
1986	Challenger disaster
1989	Atlantis shuttle sends probe Magellan to Venus

Washington, D.C., Visit, page 85
1. During the War of 1812 the mansion was burned by the British. The stonework was painted white to cover the black scars of the flames.
2. The god Mercury. Bronze.
3. There was a political quarrel about the monument in 1854 while it was being built. It stood incomplete at 153 feet for 25

years. When work resumed, the stone used was of a different color and the earlier stone had weathered.

4. 555 feet from the base to the top.
5. The Vietnam Veterans Memorial
6. No.
7. The names of the first 48 states, Lincoln's second inaugural address, and the Gettysburg Address.
8. "We hold these truths to be self-evident, that all men are created equal, that they are endowed by their Creator with certain unalienable rights, that among these are life, liberty, and the pursuit of happiness."
9. White Georgia marble
10. The Tomb of the Unknown Soldier

Zoo Excursion: Birds, pages 91–93
TYPES OF BEAKS
Answers might include

- Fish-eating beak: heron, gull, black skipper
- Insect-catching beak: nighthawk, swift, swallow, chickadee, flycatcher
- Insect- and fruit-eating beak: in the tropics—parrot, hornbill, toucan; in cooler climates—catbird, mockingbird, robin, waxwing
- Seed-eating beak: sparrow, grosbeak, finch
- Water- and mud-sifting beak: duck, goose, swan
- Chisel beak: woodpecker, flicker, nuthatch
- Preying beak: hawk, owl, eagle, falcon
- Probing beak: killdeer, brown creeper, hummingbird

TYPES OF FEET
Answers might include

- Preying feet: hawk, owl, falcon
- Perching feet: wren, bluebird, robin, all other songbirds
- Climbing feet: nuthatch, flicker, all woodpeckers
- Wading feet: killdeer, plover, sandpiper
- Swimming feet—webbed version: duck, goose, loon
- Swimming feet—lobed version: horned grebe, coot

Zoo Excursion: Mammals and Reptiles, pages 94–95
There are many kinds of animals to observe at the zoo. With the student (and parents, if de-sired), select activities appropriate for the student's age and for the zoo.

CAMELS

1. The fur is thickest on the top of the hump. It provides insulation against the sun's heat. The hump is a large lump of fat, or stored food, from which the camel can draw nourishment if food is hard to find.
2. The camel has bigger feet. The camel often walks over desert, and larger feet make it easier for the camel to walk over desert sand.
3. The camel has thick eyebrows that protect its eyes from blowing sand or dust.

CHIMPANZEES, MONKEYS, AND APES

1. *Answers might include the following:*
   - Chimpanzees care for their young by picking through each other's fur to remove any dirt, leeches, or insects. Monkey mothers care for their young by nursing them from a few weeks to two years, depending on the species. The young monkey hangs onto its mother almost from the time of birth by grasping her fur. Apes care for their young by hunting for food for them.
2. *Answers might include the following:*
   - Young chimps help each other. Monkeys stay by their mothers from birth. Young apes act as though they do not care about their parents.

GIRAFFES

1. The giraffe's main color is tawny (light brownish-yellow).
2. The advantage of the broken color pattern is that it camouflages giraffes, or makes them difficult to see when they are standing among the trees.
3. The giraffe's height is an advantage when reaching for food in high trees. It also helps the giraffe see danger coming.
4. The number of horns ranges from two to five. They actually aren't horns; they are bony lumps on the skull and are covered with hair. Their scientific name is "ossicones." The hair is often rubbed off the male's horns, because male giraffes butt heads during contests to see who is stronger.
5. The tongue is very long. When feeding, the giraffe strips the leaves off branches with its tongue. The tongue moves side to side in a circular motion.

6. The giraffe escapes from predators by running. When one giraffe sees danger, it makes no sound; it just begins to run. This is a sign to the others that there is danger. Their running gait is actually a gallop. It is difficult for giraffes to run, however, and they stop running as soon as the danger is over.
7. The giraffe's foot is much larger.

REPTILES

1. A cold-blooded animal is one whose body temperature changes as the temperature of its environment changes.
2. *This answer will vary depending on the zoo's collection. Some large reptiles are alligators, crocodiles, boa constrictors, and king snakes.*
3. A lizard's eyes open and close; a snake's do not. Most lizards have legs; snakes do not. More snakes than lizards are poisonous; the only poisonous lizards are gila monsters and leaded lizards. Snakes have fangs; lizards do not.
4. Reptiles have scaly skin. Lizards and snakes shed their skin and grow new skin as they get larger.

SEALS AND SEA LIONS

1. Seals have hair on their bodies like all mammals do. They breathe air, so they need to come to the surface of the water often when they are swimming. It might be possible to see a mother seal nursing her baby as all female mammals do.
2. Body shape

3. All seals have slitlike nostrils, which they close when they dive or swim under water. Most seals can see and hear well, but they have a poor sense of smell.
4. *Answers will vary.*

REFERENCES

Abruscato, Joe, and Jack Hassard. *The Whole Cosmos: Catalog of Science Activities for Kids of All Ages*. Glenview, IL: Scott Foresman, 1977.

Brown, Joseph E. *Wonders of Seals and Sea Lions*. New York: Dodd, Mead, 1976.

Brown, Tom, Jr. *Tom Brown's Guide to Wild Edible and Medicinal Plants*. New York: Berkley Books, 1985.

Chandler, David. *Exploring the Night Sky with Binoculars*. LaVerne, CA: David Chandler Press, 1983.

French, Dr. Bevan M. *What's New on the Moon*. Washington, DC: NASA, U.S. Government Printing Office, 1980.

Gurrey, Geren. *Walk in Space*. New York: Random House, 1967.

Jason, Dan. *Your Own Food: A Forager's Guide*. Vancouver, British Columbia: Intermedia, 1979.

Kopp, O. W., et al. *Elementary School Aerospace Activities*. Washington, DC: NASA, U.S. Government Printing Office, 1984.

Long, John E. *Our Nation's Capital*. Garden City, NY: Doubleday, 1975.

MacRobert, Alan. "Pathfinding in the Sky." *Sky and Telescope*. July 1986.

McCormack, Alan, ed. *Outdoor Areas as Learning Laboratories: CESI Sourcebook*. Columbus, OH: ERIC Clearinghouse for Science, Mathematics, and Environmental Education, 1982.

McGowen, Tom. *Album of Astronomy*. New York: Macmillan, 1979.

Mallison, George, et al. *Silver Burdett Science 6*. Morristown, NJ: Silver Burdett, 1984.

NASA. *Life Aboard the Space Shuttle*. NASA Facts. Kennedy Space Center, FL: J. F. Kennedy Space Center, 1982.

Palmer, Bill. *History of Electronics*. Radio Shack, a division of Tandy Corporation, 1987. Brochure.

Peterson, Roger Torey. *The Birds*. New York: Time, 1963.

Podendorf, Illa, ed. *Sun, Moon, and Stars: A New True Book*. Chicago: Children's Press, 1981.

Schlein, Miriam, and Betty Fraser. *Giraffe, The Silent Giant*. Soquel, CA: Four Winds Press, 1976.

Scobee, Dick, and June Scobee. "An Astronaut Speaks." *Science and Children*. March 1986.

Stone, Sally F. "Illinois Birds." *Nature Discovery I*. Springfield, IL: Illinois Department of Conservation, Nature Discovery Press, 1986.

Thier, Herbert, et al. *Scientific Theories*. Chicago: Rand McNally, 1978.

Voris, Helen, et al. *Teach the Mind, Touch the Spirit: A Guide to Focused Field Trips*. Chicago: Field Museum of Natural History, 1986.

Wexo, John Bonnett. *Giraffe: Zoobooks*. San Diego: Wildlife Education, 1983.

World Book Encyclopedia. Chicago: Field Enterprises, 1987.

Yount, Lisa. *The Telescope*. New York: Walker, 1983.

Activities

Vacation Assignment Contract

I, _____ , agree to complete the
Log Book and the Travel Data plus the following activities while on my vacation:

_____

_____

_____

I will

1. read and follow all directions,

2. bring back a finished product, including the log book and pamphlets from places visited (if they are available), on the date requested by my teacher,

3. allow my family to advise me, but do the work I turn in by myself, and

4. take my time to do this assignment correctly—and still *go and have a good time!*

Evaluation criteria:

_____

_____

_____

Signed,

_____
(student's signature)

_____
(signature of accompanying adult)

_____
(teacher's signature)

Log Book Instructions

Use a spiral notebook or a binder for the log book for your trip. DO NOT USE THE NOTEBOOK FOR ANYTHING ELSE. Always use your best penmanship. Use only a blue or black pen or pencil, except for special features that need to be colored. You may record any interesting information in your log book, but it should contain the following items:

1. *A map of the states or countries you visit.* Label the states or countries. Use arrows or a colored line to show your travel route. If you go by car or train, draw lines between each city you pass through. If you are flying, the airline magazine at each passenger's seat will show the route.

2. *Make a list of the cities where you stop.* Find out the population of each one. Make a data table showing the cities from the least populated to the most populated.

3. *Record each day's events.* Be sure to include the date, a time line of events, and the weather conditions.

4. *Note the following items (if appropriate) as you travel:*
   a. type of field crops
   b. type of animals
   c. type of land
   d. type of houses
   e. people you meet
   f. any other interesting information you wish to include

5. *Calculate the number of miles you have traveled and determine the gas mileage at the end of each day.* (See "Travel Data.")
   If you travel by plane, train, bus, or ship, ask the pilot, flight attendant, engineer, driver, or captain the number of miles you have traveled and the number of gallons of fuel used. Determine the fuel consumption in miles per gallon.

6. *Conduct and write down two interviews with new people you meet.*

     The first interview should be with someone you meet while you are traveling to your destination (if you fly, the pilot or flight attendant would be interesting to interview, for example). Ask about his or her job, how long he or she has done that work, what training was needed, and any other questions that will give you more information about the job. Plan your questions before you do the interview.

     The second interview should be with someone you meet at your vacation site. It can be about the person's job or about another topic of interest.

7. *When you reach your destination, do the activity or activities you have contracted to do.* Record the information in your log book. (Each activity sheet identifies the information to be recorded in your log book with the symbol ✏ .)

     For some excursions, it may be easiest to take notes on your observations on the activity sheet. Later, you can neatly transfer the information to your log book. Or, if you are going to answer a set of questions about a number of different animals, you might want to make several copies of those questions in your log book before you start your investigation so that you can easily record the answers during your tour.

8. *If there are pamphlets or other types of free information about places you visit, be sure to collect them and add them to your log book.*

9. *And add anything else—such as pictures, poems, or stories—to make your log book more meaningful to you.*

Name _____

Travel Data

Departure date: _____ Return date: _____

Type(s) of transportation: _____

Family members on trip: _____

_____

For each mode of transportation you use during your vacation, fill in the data in the appropriate section below. If you travel only by car on your vacation, you need to fill in only the information under "By Automobile" and record the daily hours and miles of travel in your log book. If, for example, you fly across country and then go by car to your final destination, fill in the flight information under "By Plane" and record the daily auto travel data (under "By Automobile") in your log book.

By Automobile

Type of automobile: _____

Mileage on speedometer before departure: _____

Mileage on speedometer after return: _____

Number of gallons of gas required to fill tank: _____

✎ *Record the following information in your log book for each day of automobile travel:*

    1. Date

    2. Time of departure (local time)

    3. Place of departure

    4. Time of arrival (local time)

    5. Place of arrival

    6. Miles traveled

    7. Miles per gallon

Name _____

~~~~~~~~~~~~~~~~ **By Airplane** ~~~~~~~~~~~~~~~~

DEPARTURE

Name of airline: _____

Flight number: _____

Type of aircraft: _____

Number of people the plane can hold: _____

Number of people on your flight: _____

Number of crew members: _____

Pilot's name: _____ Flight engineer's name: _____

Flight attendants' names: _____

_____

Number of miles of flight: _____

Gallons of fuel on plane: _____ Mileage per gallon: _____

Mileage per gallon: _____

Cruising altitude: _____

Time of departure (local time): _____

Time of arrival (local time): _____

RETURN

Name of airline: _____

Flight number: _____

Type of aircraft: _____

Number of people the plane can hold: _____

Number of people on your flight: _____

Number of crew members: _____

Pilot's name: _____ Flight engineer's name: _____

Flight attendants' names: _____

_____

Number of miles of flight: _____

Gallons of fuel on plane: _____ Mileage per gallon: _____

Cruising altitude: _____

Time of departure (local time): _____

Time of arrival (local time): _____

Name _____

 **By Train**

DEPARTURE

Name of train company: _____

Number of cars on train: _____

Conductor's name: _____

Engineer's name: _____

Maximum speed of train: _____

Towns where the train stops: _____

_____

_____

Number of miles of trip: _____

Gallons of fuel on train: _____

Mileage per gallon: _____

Time of departure (local time): _____

Time of arrival (local time): _____

RETURN

Name of train company: _____

Number of cars on train: _____

Conductor's name: _____

Engineer's name: _____

Maximum speed of train: _____

Towns where the train stops: _____

_____

_____

Number of miles of trip: _____

Gallons of fuel on train: _____

Mileage per gallon: _____

Time of departure (local time): _____

Time of arrival (local time): _____

Name _____

 **By Bus**

DEPARTURE

Name of bus company: _____

Driver's name: _____

Number of gallons of gas on bus: _____

Number of miles of trip: _____

Mileage per gallon: _____

Number of people the bus can hold: _____

Number of people actually on the bus: _____

Towns where the bus stops: _____

_____

Time of departure (local time): _____

Time of arrival (local time): _____

RETURN

Name of bus company: _____

Driver's name: _____

Number of gallons of gas on bus: _____

Number of miles of trip: _____

Mileage per gallon: _____

Number of people the bus can hold: _____

Number of people actually on the bus: _____

Towns where the bus stops: _____

_____

Time of departure (local time): _____

Time of arrival (local time): _____

Name _____

∿∿∿∿∿ By Ship ∿∿∿∿∿

Name of cruise line: _____

Name of ship: _____

Name of the deck your cabin is on: _____

Captain's name: _____

Average speed of ship: _____

Miles traveled on cruise: _____

Amount of fuel carried on ship: _____

Mileage per gallon: _____

Time of departure: _____

NAME OF EACH PORT VISITED	TIME OF ARRIVAL AT PORT	TIME SPENT IN PORT
_____	_____	_____
_____	_____	_____
_____	_____	_____
_____	_____	_____
_____	_____	_____
_____	_____	_____
_____	_____	_____
_____	_____	_____
_____	_____	_____
_____	_____	_____

Favorite activity on board ship: _____

Favorite activity in port: _____

Time of return home: _____

How to Make a Display Box

Materials

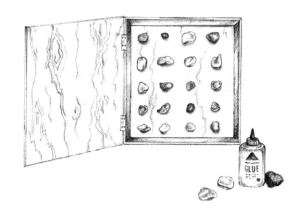

2 pieces of plywood, each about 2' x 2½'

2 strips of wood the same thickness as plywood, 3"–4" wide x 2' long

2 strips of wood the same thickness as plywood, 3"–4" wide x 2½' long

Nails

2 hinges

Handle

2 screw eyes

Hook or wire

Glue

Small box with lid

Con-Tact paper (optional)

Paint (optional)

Index cards (or other small cards to fit in small box)

Procedure

- Nail the strips of wood around the outside edges of one of the pieces of plywood. Place the second piece of plywood on top of the strips. Use the hinges to attach one of the long sides of the top piece of plywood to wood strip. (Place each hinge about 6 inches in from the end.) This will make a box with a hinged lid. (You can paint the box if you wish to.)

- Attach the handle in the center of the long strip of wood opposite the hinges. Glue the small box in one of the inside corners of the display box. (You can cover the small box with Con-Tact paper if you like.) This box will hold identification cards to describe what is in the display.

- Screw one screw eye into the top of the lid above the handle. Screw the other screw eye into the wood strip above the handle. Attach the hook or wire to one screw eye, and use to keep the box closed while carrying it.

- Arrange in the box the items that you wish to display. When you have an arrangement that pleases you, glue each item securely inside the bottom of the box. Label each item with a letter, number, or one- or two-word description. Make an index card for each item by putting the item's label at the top of the card and then describing or explaining the item. Put the cards in the small box.

- Now your display is ready to go!

Amusement Park Visit: Centripetal Force

Objective: To observe the effect of centripetal force while on an amusement park ride.

Materials

    Baby bottle (clear plastic)
    Lead sinker
    String
    Rubber band
    Log book
    Pencil

Procedure

The word *centripetal* comes from two Latin words meaning "to seek the center." Centripetal force compels a body to move in a circular path. The law of inertia states that, in the absence of outside forces, an object moves in a straight line at a constant speed. An outside force must act on an object to make it move in a curved path.

- Tie one end of the string to the lead sinker.
- Tie the other end of the string through the nipple of the baby bottle so that the sinker is on the outside of the nipple. (You may need to enlarge the hole in the nipple so that the string will go through.)
- Place the sinker inside the baby bottle. The nipple will be inverted in the bottle, and the sinker will be hanging inside the bottle. The string should be long enough so that the sinker can swing freely. Screw the top ring on the bottle.
- Use the rubber band to hold the bottle to your wrist. (If you don't do this, the bottle will fly away during your ride.)
- Go on a ride that will turn you upside down.
- Observe what happens to the sinker as you go upside down.

After the ride, record the following information in your log book.

1. What happened to the sinker?
2. Why do you think this happened?
3. Draw a diagram of what happened.
4. Describe your feelings or sensations while on the ride.
5. Give other examples of centripetal force.

Go and Have a Good Time © 1990 Fearon Teacher Aids

Amusement Park Visit: The Coriolis Force

Objective: To see the Coriolis force while on the round-up (the ride that presses the riders' bodies against the side as it spins and the floor drops).

Materials
Nerf balls
Camera (optional)
Log book
Pencil

Procedure

The Coriolis force (sometimes called the Coriolis effect or the Coriolis acceleration) is the tendency of any body on or above the surface of the earth to move sideways because of the rotation of the earth. In the Northern Hemisphere, the drift is toward the right, and in the Southern Hemisphere, the drift is toward the left. This force was first identified by the French scientist Gaspard G. Coriolis (1792–1843).

- You will need three or more people for the activity—at least one observer and one pair of riders.

- ASK THE RIDE OPERATOR PERMISSION TO DO THE ACTIVITY.

- Two people get on the ride and stand directly across from each other. (If additional pairs of people take part, each person should be directly across from his or her partner.) Each rider should hold one nerf ball and can carry extras in a pocket, if desired.

- Before the ride starts, decide who will throw the first ball.

- If possible, a third person (and more, if desired) stands above the ride to watch what happens.

- After the ride is at full speed, throw the nerf ball to your partner. Do this a few times.

The observer records in the log book what happens. (The observer can also take pictures.)

1. What happens to the nerf balls?
2. What causes this to happen?
3. How does this phenomenon relate to the earth and space travel?

Amusement Park Visit: Pulse Rate

Objective: To observe the effect of amusement park rides on the pulse rate.

Materials

    Stopwatch or watch with a second hand

    Log book

    Pencil

Procedure

Take your pulse while you are resting, and record it in the log book. To find your pulse rate per minute, count the number of beats for 15 seconds and multiply that number by four.

- Select a ride to go on. Check your pulse rate again while you are waiting in line. Record this pulse rate in the log book.

- If possible, take your pulse while on the ride—and remember to record it after the ride.

- Take your pulse once more right after the ride is over. Record this pulse rate in the log book.

- Repeat this process for a number of rides.

After the rides, add the following information to your log book.

1. Prepare a data table with your information. Your table should be set up similar to the one below.

Pulse Rates Before, During, and After Amusement Park Rides

Ride	Pulse Rate		
	Waiting	Riding	After
Rollercoaster	_____	_____	_____
Ferris wheel	_____	_____	_____

> *Extra Credit:* Prepare a bar graph or line graph comparing one category of pulse rate for all the rides you went on.

2. Describe your feelings while waiting for and being on each ride.
3. Which ride caused the highest pulse rate? Can you explain why?

Go and Have a Good Time © 1990 Fearon Teacher Aids

Aquarium Visit

Objectives: To learn facts about aquatic life found in an aquarium.

To gain information about the operation of an aquarium (optional).

Materials

    Drawing equipment
    Camera
    Log book
    Pencil

Procedure

Most aquariums have aquatic creatures from all over the world. Try to select a good variety of animals for this activity.

Select the number of animals you will observe and report on.

Number: _____

For each exhibit, record the following information in your log book:

1. Name of the animal (or animals)
2. Native area (such as Pacific Ocean)
3. Type of water (salt or fresh)

For each animal, record the following information:

4. Length
5. Width
6. Weight
7. Colors
8. Special markings
9. Special features
10. Interesting facts

Make or obtain a picture of each animal you observe. You can

- draw pictures of the animals,
- take pictures of the exhibits, or
- buy postcards or slides of the animals.

Upon your return to school, be prepared to show the class your pictures and to share the information you have gained about the aquatic animals you observed.

In your log book, write a poem or story about one or more of the animals you observed.

> *Extra Credit:* Interview a staff member at the aquarium to find out about its operation. Record the interview in your log book.

Beach Exploration

Objective: To see what sand is made of.

Materials
- Small tray
- Hand lens
- Sifting device, such as a piece of wire screen
- Magnet
- Crayons or colored pencils
- Camera (optional)
- Log book
- Pencil

Procedure
- Go to a beach. Scoop up a handful of sand and smooth it out on the tray.
- Look at the sand with a hand lens.
- Sift the sand to separate the fine grains from the larger ones and from shells, bits of wood, and other objects.
- Use the magnet to see if there is any metal in the sand.
- Test other samples of sand from different places on the beach to get a variety of examples.

 Record in your log book the different colors of sand and how they were formed. Use the table "Types of Sand" to determine the origin of the sand. Also record materials other than sand that you found.

Draw or take a picture of the beach where you have explored the sand.

 In your log book, write a short story or a poem about the beach.

Types of Sand

Color	Rock Source	Shape	How Formed
Pink or red	Granite	Egg	Tumbled by glacial and wave action, worn and chipped
Glassy white	Quartz	Egg	
Flat black	Shale or slate	Smooth, angled	Hard rock carried by glaciers
Gray	Limestone	Flat, round	Sedimentary rocks worn by water and weather
Gray & black	Schist	Flat, round	
Green or milky white	Glass	Flat, round	Rounded as pieces tumble against each other

It is also possible to find

- coral embedded in limestone
- small fossils
- black, porous chunks of coke from ships' boilers
- metal

Go and Have a Good Time © 1990 Fearon Teacher Aids

Bird Watching

Objective: To observe birds in your vacation area.

Materials

    Bird book
    Binoculars
    Camera (optional)
    Tape recorder (optional)
    Log book
    Pencil

Procedure

Go for a walk—in the early morning if possible. Take along your bird book and binoculars. Bring a camera, too, if you want to take some pictures.

- Quietly walk through the woods or other area you have chosen for bird observation.
- Use your bird book to help you identify the birds you see.

✏️ In your log book,

1. write the names and descriptions of each type of bird you see;

2. if you see any types of birds more than once, record the number of times you see each type; and

3. describe the actions of the birds and what they eat, and, if you can spot the nests of any of them, describe those, too.

If possible, take pictures of the birds to share with the class on your return.

(Optional) Use a tape recorder to capture the calls of birds.

Cave Exploration

Objective: To become more aware of a cave.

Materials
    Camera
    Log book
    Pencil

Procedure

As you tour the cave, try to find the answers to the following questions. Record them in your log book.

1. Who discovered the cave?

2. How was it discovered?

3. When was it discovered?

4. How large is the cave?

5. How old is the cave?

6. What kind of rock is found in the cave?

7. What causes the stalactites and stalagmites?

8. Are the stalactites and stalagmites still getting larger? If so, how can you tell?

9. What causes different colors in the formations?

10. Is there any plant life in the cave? If so, where? What are the sources of nourishment for the plants?

11. What is the largest structure in the cave?

12. What is the temperature in the cave?

13. Is there any animal life in the cave? If so, tell some interesting facts about what kinds of adaptations these animals have for living in the cave.

After your tour of the cave is over, add the following to your log book:

14. a paragraph describing your feelings while you were in the cave,

15. a story or poem about your cave visit, and

16. any other interesting facts about the cave you visited.

Cemetery Exploration

Objective: To observe a cemetery from a new point of view.

Materials

    Dark-color crayons with paper removed

    Large sheets of plain paper

    Metric tape measure

    "Types of Cemetery Monuments" chart
      (pages 37–38)

    Rocks

    Rock identification book

    Log book

    Pencil

Procedure

With your teacher, select the activities that you will do on your tour of the cemetery. Check each activity you select in the box by the activity name.

TOMBSTONE GEOLOGY

Collect rocks in the area. Use the rock identification book to identify them.

    Look through the cemetery to see if any of the tombstones are like any of the rocks you have collected.

✏️ In your log book,

  1. describe the rock and the cemetery marker (be sure to include colors and other features such as weathering), and

  2. name the type of rock that makes the best cemetery marker and explain why.

TYPES OF MONUMENTS

✏️ Look at the chart "Types of Cemetery Monuments." In your log book,

  1. record how many of each kind of monument you saw, and

  2. make a bar graph or data table to show this information.

TOMBSTONE ART

Use the side of a crayon on the paper to make rubbings of engravings on the tombstones. Combine several designs on one sheet of paper for an interesting picture.

TOMBSTONE MATH

✏️ Find the following information by observation or calculation, and record it in your log book:

1. the date of the oldest tombstone,
2. the date of the newest tombstone, and
3. the ages of several people when they died.

TOMBSTONE HISTORY

The grave of a veteran of a war can be marked in one of two ways. It is sometimes marked with a metal stake that has a star on the top, and the stake is placed beside the cemetery marker. Engraved on this star are the war the veteran was in and the years in which the veteran served. Another method of marking a veteran's grave is a rectangular plate either placed flat on the ground or attached to the cemetery marker. It states the person's name, date of birth and death, rank in the service, and the war in which he or she served.

✏️ Look for markers of veterans of wars. In your log book,

1. draw pictures of different types of markers, and
2. make a data table or graph to show the number of persons in the cemetery who fought in each war.

TOMBSTONE GEOMETRY

✏️ After you do the following activities, record the data in your log book.

1. Measure the width, length, and thickness of several markers.
2. Calculate the volume of each of those markers.

CEMETERY HISTORY

✏️ Interview the caretaker of the cemetery or someone else who knows its history. Record the interesting facts in your log book.

Types of Cemetery Monuments

CROSS

- May be any height or size
- May be made of any type of stone

GOTHIC

- Average height is about 90 cm
- Usually made of marble
- Has a pointed arch

OBELISK

- Vertical shaft, up to 150 cm high
- Usually made of marble
- Sometimes topped with an orb or other symbol
- Popular around 1890–1920

CROSS-VAULT OBELISK

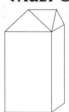

- Like the Obelisk, but with a vaulted roof and no point

TABLET

- Vertical slab with round arched top, up to 70 cm wide by 90 cm high
- Made of marble or granite
- Sometimes found in pairs to represent the tablets on which the Ten Commandments were inscribed

PULPIT

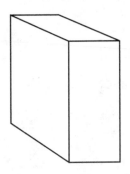

- Vertical slab with an average height of 75 cm
- Made of marble or granite
- Vertical face for the inscription is usually slate
- Sometimes an open Bible is on the top

SCROLL

- Average height is 30 cm
- Usually made of granite
- Always horizontal

BLOCK

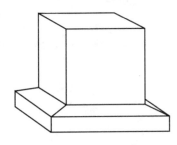

- Average height is 60 cm
- Usually made of granite
- Sometimes has a rounded top
- First used around 1920

RAISED TOP

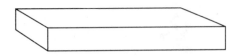

- Horizontal slab with an average height of 15 cm
- Inscription is on the top

LAWN PLAQUE

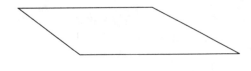

- Flush with the ground
- Made of granite or metal
- Used since 1940

City, Town, or Village Excursion

Objective: To gain important facts about a city, town, or village that is visited.

Materials

Camera or drawing pencils and paper
Log book
Pencil

Procedure

Record the following information in your log book:

1. Name of city, town, or village

2. Is it a city, a town, or a village?

3. Population

4. When was it founded?

5. How old is it?

6. What are the major highways?

7. What are the major railroads (if any)?

8. What are the major airports (if any)?

9. What are the major bodies of water nearby?

Draw or take pictures of your favorite sights.

Select one of the following topics for an oral report (with pictures—slides, snapshots, drawings, or postcards) that you will give after you return to class:

● How the city, town, or village was founded and interesting historical facts about it

● How one major industry operates (visit a factory or farm to collect information)

Color in Your World

Objective: To observe and record the colors seen while traveling.

Materials

"Color Wheel" chart

Markers or crayons

Log book

Pencil

Procedure

As you travel, record the names of objects you see in the appropriate place on the Color Wheel page. Discuss with your teacher how long to spend doing this observation.

For example, you might record "roses" in the red section, "oranges" in the orange section, "sunflowers" in the yellow section, "grass" in the green section, "sky" in the blue section, and "grapes" in the violet section.

✏️ In your log book, make a bar graph to record the number of times you saw each color.

✏️ As you travel, keep a data table in your log book of the various colors of cars that you see. At the top of the table, make a column heading for each color (red, orange, yellow, green, blue, violet) plus black, white, gray, and brown. Place a mark in the column below the color each time you see a car of that color.

Go and Have a Good Time © 1990 Fearon Teacher Aids

Name _____

Color Wheel I

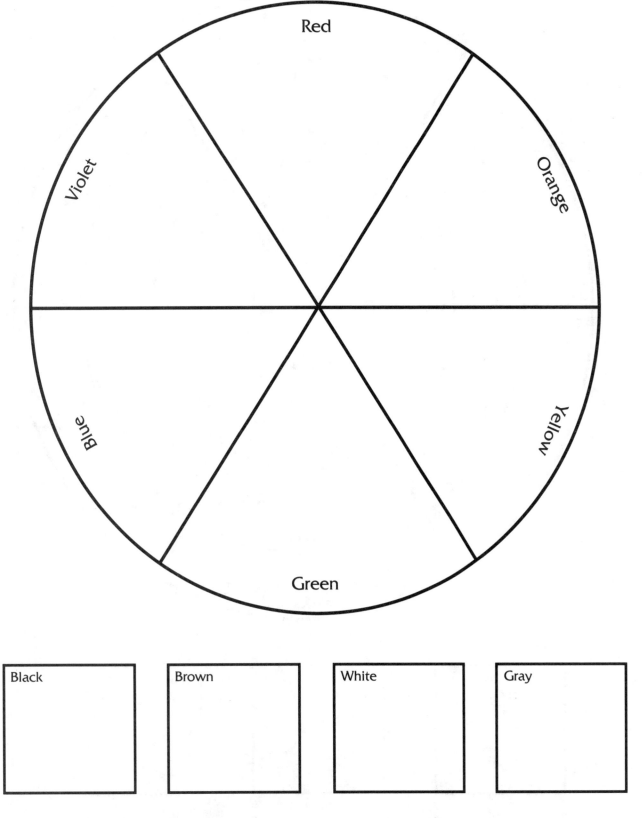

Name _____

Color Wheel II

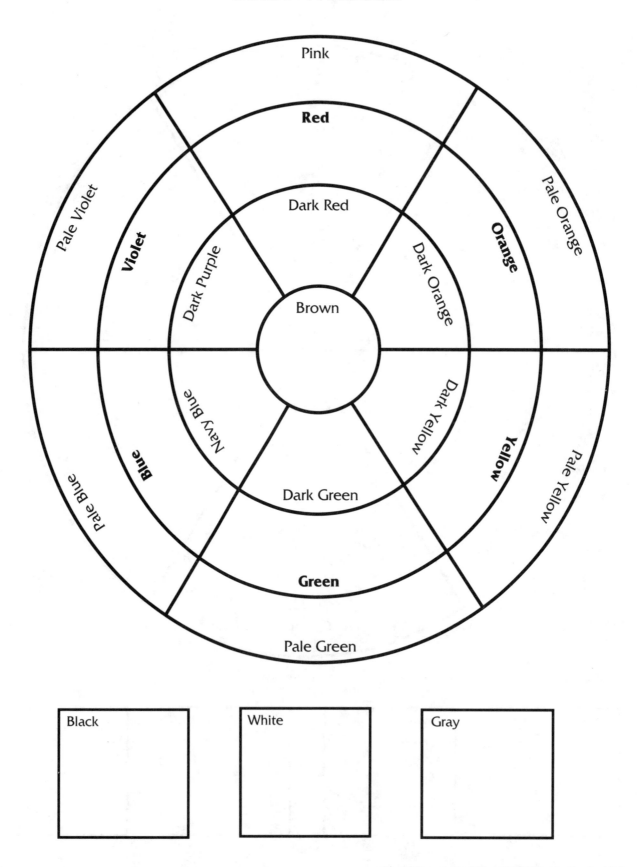

Black

White

Gray

Color My World with Snow

Objective: To observe and record how color affects the melting rate of snow.

Materials

Paper or tiles in several different
    colors (such as black, white,
    red, blue, green, yellow)
Snow
Watch
Measuring cup
Graph paper
Log book
Pencil

Procedure

This experiment should be done on a sunny day when there is snow on the ground.

- Place the pieces of paper or tiles on a flat surface outside, such as a driveway or sidewalk.

- With the measuring cup, measure equal amounts of snow. Place the same amount of snow on each piece of paper or tile.

In your log book, note the time that you place the snow on the paper or tiles. Then, predict the order in which the snow will melt on the pieces of paper or the tiles.

- Use the watch to record the time when each pile of snow melts, and then figure out how long it took for each pile to melt.

In your log book, record the order in which the piles of snow melted and the amount of time it took for each one to melt.

In your log book, prepare a bar graph of the results.

Factory Visit

Objective: To learn how a specific product is manufactured.

Materials

    Camera (optional)
    Log book
    Pencil

Procedure

✎ During a visit to a factory, find out the following information and record it in your log book:

1. the name of the factory

2. how many people work in the factory

3. the factory's product (name and description)

4. the steps used to manufacture the product

5. the components of the product

6. where those components come from

7. how the finished product is used

✎ Add any other interesting information that you learn during your visit to the factory.

- If possible, bring a sample of the product back to school for the rest of the class to see, use, or enjoy.

- If it is permitted, take photos or slides of the various parts of the factory. Share them with the class.

          Go and Have a Good Time © 1990 Fearon Teacher Aids

Farm Visit

Objective: To observe the behavior of farm animals.

Materials

    Camera or drawing materials
    Log book
    Pencil

Procedure

On a visit to a farm, select a number of animals to observe during the day.

In your log book, record the following information:

1. the behavior of the animals in the morning, during the day, and at night;

2. comparisons and contrasts between several pairs of animals (for example, you could describe how a cow and a horse are alike and different); and

3. a bar graph showing the types of animals and the number of each type.

Take photographs or draw pictures of the animals to illustrate the information in your log book.

Fishing Trip

Objective: To observe and record the details of a fresh-water, salt-water, or deep-sea fishing trip.

Materials

Fish identification book
Fishing gear
Thermometer
Metric ruler
Camera (optional)
Log book
Pencil

Procedure

✏️ Use your log book to record the following information.

1. Give the location of your fishing trip.

2. Describe the area where you are fishing. Include such information as the types of trees and other vegetation and the depth of the water—and, if you are fishing in a lake, give its area.

3. Record the weather conditions. Describe the clouds. Estimate the wind speed. Use the thermometer to measure the air and water temperatures.

4. Explain the fishing procedure. Include such information as the type of pole, the depth of the line, the type of bait, why that particular bait was selected, and how it was obtained.

✏️ After catching each fish (good luck!), record the following information in your log book.

5. Describe the fish's behavior.

6. Use the metric ruler to measure its length in centimeters.

7. Use the fish identification book to identify the type of fish.

8. Make a data table of the different kinds of fish (or the different sizes if they were all of one kind) caught on your fishing trip.

Use slides, snapshots, drawings, or postcards to help record this trip.

Geology Comparison

Objective: To compare the rocks in an area to those used as construction material in buildings, monuments, and roads of a nearby city or village.

Materials

Rock identification book
Box for collecting rocks
Camera (optional)
Poster board
Super glue
Log book
Pencil

Procedure

- Take a walk through the countryside near a city or village. Collect a small specimen of each of the different kinds of rock you see.

- Use the rock identification book to identify the types of rocks.

- Go for a walk through the city or village. Take your rock collection along, and match the rocks in your collection to the rocks used in the buildings, monuments, and roads.

✏️ In your log book, make a data table to show the various structures that are made out of each type of rock. Your data table might begin like this:

TYPE OF ROCK	STRUCTURE	IDENTIFYING PROPERTIES
Granite	City Hall	Pink rock with black and gray flecks

- Make a labeled poster of the rocks to display in the classroom. You might also take pictures (or buy postcards) of the structures that are built out of the various rocks and add those to the poster.

Hammered Leaf and Flower Prints

Objectives: To preserve leaf and flower prints from the vacation site.

　　To identify the leaves and flowers collected.

Materials

Fresh green leaves

Flowers

Hammer (don't pack in carry-on luggage if you are flying to your vacation site)

Tablespoon measure

Container for water

Small paintbrush

Ferrous sulfate (can be found at drugstores and art supply stores)

100% cotton muslin

Waxed paper

Newspaper

Tree and flower identification books

Log book

Pencil

Procedure

Collect several different kinds of leaves and flowers from your vacation area. Pick only one or two of each kind, so that there will be some left for others to enjoy. (Don't pick flowers if it's forbidden at your vacation site!)

Use the tree and flower identification books to identify what you have picked. Record the names of the plants (with sketches if you wish) in your log book.

- Place several sheets of newspaper on flat ground. Put the muslin on top of the newspaper.

- Arrange the leaves and flowers on the muslin. Do not crowd or overlap them.

- Place the waxed paper on top of the leaves and flowers.

- Hold the hammer 2 or 3 inches above the leaves and flowers, and use quick, firm strokes to gently pound them into the fabric. Begin at the center of each leaf or flower, and pound in a spiral until you have pounded the entire leaf or flower.

- Let the leaves and flowers dry, and then peel off the waxed paper.

- Remove the dry leaf and flower flakes.

- Mix 1 tablespoon of ferrous sulfate in a pint of water.

- Paint each leaf or flower print immediately with this solution to preserve the print.

- Let the solution set for at least two minutes, and then rinse the muslin in cool water.

- The muslin can be used for a tablecloth, a wall hanging, or a skirt. Or you can cut it into squares and use the pieces for a quilt.

Lake Exploration

Objective: To become familiar with a lake and its environment.

Materials

Fish identification book

Plant identification book

Thermometer

Long string or fishing line

Felt-tip pens or colored pencils

Drawing paper

Camera (optional)

Log book

Pencil

Procedure

✏️ Research the answers to the following questions, and record them in your log book.

1. What is the name of the lake?
2. What is the length of the lake?
3. What is the width of the lake?
4. What is the maximum depth of the lake?
5. What is the origin of the lake?
6. What types of vegetation grow in the lake?
7. What types of fish are found in the lake?
8. What types of vegetation grow on the shores of the lake?
9. What types of animals live around the lake?
10. What types of boats are found on the lake?
11. What do you predict the temperature of the water is just below the surface? (Make this prediction before you go on to the next question.)
12. What is the temperature of the water just below the surface? (Use the thermometer to measure the water temperature.)
13. What do you predict the temperature of the water is at the bottom of the lake? (Make this prediction before you go on to the next question.)
14. What is the temperature of the water at the bottom of the lake? (Securely tie the thermometer to the string or fishing line and lower it to the bottom of the lake to measure the temperature there.)

✏️ Go to a quiet spot beside the lake. In your log book, describe the lake and your feelings about being there. Compare these feelings to the feelings you have while riding in a boat.

Making Dyes

Objective: To make dye from vegetation found in the vacation area and to dye fabric with this dye.

Materials

Plain white fabric, such as a T-shirt or broadcloth for making place mats or napkins

Large pot

Measuring cup

Heat source

Water

Sieve or piece of muslin for straining dye

Pail or pan for rinsing

Wooden spoon

Dye source (see list below)

Procedure

- In the large pot, boil 1 cup of the selected dye source in 2 cups of water for 10–15 minutes. Let it cool.
- Strain this mixture through the sieve or piece of muslin.
- Return the liquid dye to the pot.
- Place the fabric to be dyed into the pot. (To make an interesting pattern, you can tie the fabric so that parts of it will not contact the dye.)
- Bring the liquid to a boil, and stir gently with the wooden spoon so that the fabric is evenly dyed. (Note: Cotton can be dyed in cold water, but the results are not as colorful.)
- When the fabric reaches the color desired, drain the liquid. Rinse the fabric in cold water to set the dye.

Record in your log book information about where the plants were found. Follow the example below.

PLANT	LOCATION	FABRIC SAMPLE
Grape	Woods in Illinois	*(drawing or a small piece of fabric, such as unbleached muslin, dyed with the shirt or other material)*

Vegetable Dye Sources

TYPE OF PLANT	PART OF PLANT	DYE COLOR
purple grapes	fruit	pink
beets	roots	red
bloodroot	root	red
elderberries	berries	red
birch	leaves	yellow
nettles*	roots and leaves	yellow
onions	brown outer layers	yellow
spinach	leaves	green
red cabbage	cabbage leaves	blue-violet
blueberries	berries	purple
butternuts	husks	purple
red cedar	bark and berries	khaki
black walnuts	nut husks	brown

* Be sure to wear gloves when collecting nettles.

Metamorphosis of Snow

Objective: To see how snow changes as it melts.

Materials

    Snow

    Hand lens

    Paper

    Log book

    Pencil

Procedure

This experiment should be done on a sunny day when there is snow on the ground.

Place some snow on a sidewalk or other flat surface outdoors.

Gently scrape some snowflakes onto a stick or other cold, dark-colored object, and look at them through the hand lens.

✎ Sketch the flakes in your log book.

Use the hand lens to continue observing the snow as it melts.

✎ Draw pictures in your log book of the flakes at several points during their melting.

✎ In your log book, describe how the snowflakes changed as they melted.

Mountain Excursion

Objective: To become more aware of the different types of mountains.

Materials

Camera or drawing materials
"Types of Mountains and Volcanoes" chart (pages 53–54)
Reference book on mountains

Rock identification book
Log book
Pencil

Procedure

Draw a picture or take a photograph of the mountains you are visiting.
Collect rocks from the mountains, and use the rock identification book to identify them.

Use the chart "Types of Mountains and Volcanoes" and the reference book on mountains to answer the following questions. Record the answers in your log book.

1. Are the mountains young or old? How can you tell? See if you can find out how old they are.
2. Which explorers first saw these mountains?
3. What type of mountain or mountain range are you viewing? Domed, folded, or fault-block mountains? Or is it an island, continental, or hot-spot volcano? What characteristics helped you make the identification?

How long would it take you to walk to the top of the highest mountain at your vacation site? First, find out how many feet high the mountain is. Then determine how many feet you walk in a minute. Divide the altitude of the mountain (in feet) by the number of feet you walk in a minute. Then divide that number by 60 to find the number of hours it would take you to get to the top of the mountain. (You may want to make an adjustment for the difference in speed between walking and climbing, or you may want to determine how fast you *climb* in a minute by climbing a nearby hill.) Record your calculations in the log book.

Find out what type of plant life is on the mountain. Does it differ at different altitudes? Record the information about plant life in your log book.

Find out what kinds of animals live on the mountain. Do different kinds live at different altitudes? Record the information about animal life in your log book.

(Optional) If one of the mountains at your vacation site is an active volcano, find out when it last erupted. What were the results of the eruption? Record the information about the volcano in your log book.

In your log book, write a story or poem about a mountain or the mountain range at your vacation site.

TYPES OF MOUNTAINS AND VOLCANOES

Folded Mountains are formed when two plates carrying continents collide and the crust of each plate folds. As the plates continue to push against each other, the mountains rise higher. Folded mountains can also form when an ocean plate pushes into a continental plate. The Himalayas were formed in this manner.

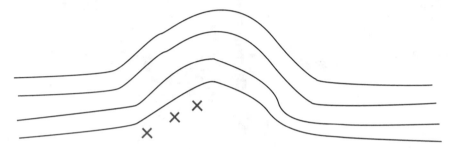

Fault-block Mountains are formed along a fault in the crust of the earth. Blocks of crust on one side of a fault push up while the other side slides down. The Teton Range in Wyoming is an example of fault-block mountains.

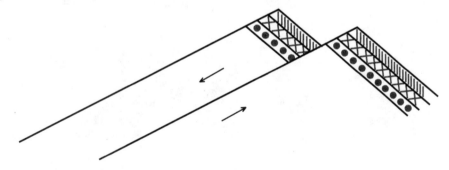

Domed Mountains are formed when magma is forced up under the crust but does not come through the surface. This type of mountain has a rounded top and a wide base. Stone Mountain near Atlanta, Georgia, is this type of mountain.

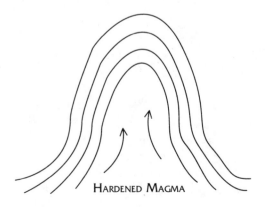

HARDENED MAGMA

Island Volcanoes are formed when two ocean plates collide. One sinks under the other, melting parts of that plate. The melted rock is forced to the surface. After many years, islands are formed. The Hawaiian Islands were formed in this manner.

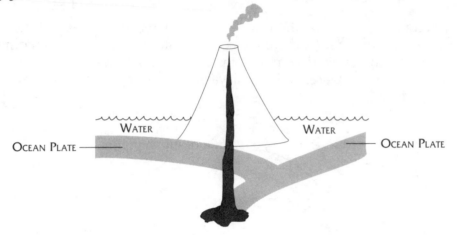

Continental Volcanoes are formed when an ocean plate sinks under a continental plate. Parts of the ocean plate melt. Some of the melted rock is forced to the surface. Mount St. Helens was formed in this way.

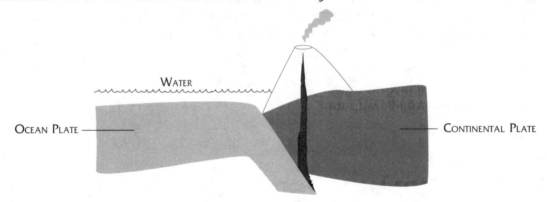

Hot-spot Volcanoes are formed in the middle of a plate. A chamber of magma forms below the surface and moves up, breaking through a weak spot in the crust. Kilauea on the island of Hawaii is a hot-spot volcano.

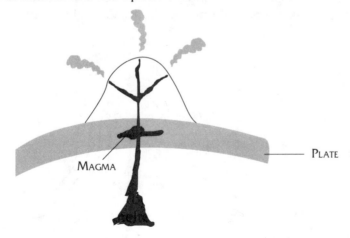

54

Music, Music, Music

Objectives: To enjoy and collect data about music while traveling.

To create songs about the trip.

Materials

Radio

Log book

Pencil

Procedure

✏️ In your log book, write the name of each song that is played on the car radio while you are traveling. Each time a song is repeated, place a mark next to the title.

✏️ When you stop, make a data table of your song list. Which song was played the most? How many songs were played only once?

If possible, listen to a different station the next day. Repeat the above steps.

✏️ In your log book, write a summary of the two data tables, comparing the two stations.

✏️ If you are tired of listening to the radio, create your own songs about your trip. Use a familiar tune or create a rap.

Here's an example of a rap.

THE FAULT-BLOCK MOUNTAINS

Cracks in the earth where the rocks have moved.

The fault blocks are back and they will never be flat.

The fault blocks are back and they will never be flat.

The Teton Range and some others too are all in a group 'cause they're fault block too.

The fault blocks are back and they will never be flat.

The fault blocks are back and they will never be flat.

Move up while the other move down. Move up while the other move down.

The fault blocks are back and they will never be flat.

National Park Excursion

Objectives: To gain information about a national park.

To share the information in a report to the class.

Materials

Camera and film (slides are best) or drawing materials

Pamphlets about the park

Log book

Pencil

Procedure

✎ Find out the answers to the following questions from the pamphlets about the park and from park rangers or other park staff. Record the answers in your log book.

1. What is the name of the park?
2. What makes this a special park?
3. Who discovered the area that is now this national park?
4. What are some special features of this national park (such as Old Faithful in Yellowstone and Half Dome in Yosemite)?
5. What kinds of animals are found in the park?
6. What kinds of trees are found in the park?
7. What kinds of flowers and small plants are found in the park?
8. What do you like best about the park? Describe it.
9. In what state (or states) is this park located?
10. What is the total area of the park?

Take slides (or a video, if possible) to illustrate the answers to as many of the questions above as possible. As you are taking the pictures, keep a record of where each one is taken and what its subject is.

Use the slides and the information entered in your log book to create a slide presentation to share with the class after your return.

✎ In your log book, write a story or poem about some aspect of your visit to the park.

Natural History Museum Visit: Dinosaurs

Objective: To become familiar with the dinosaur exhibit at a natural history museum.

Materials

Camera or drawing materials

Log book

Pencil

Procedure

Visit the museum's exhibit about dinosaurs.

Take photographs, draw pictures, or buy postcards of the various dinosaurs in the exhibit.

Find out about several kinds of dinosaurs on exhibit. Answer the following set of questions for each dinosaur by carefully studying the exhibit, using museum pamphlets, and talking to a museum guide. Record the answers in your log book.

1. What is the name of the dinosaur?

2. During what time period did it live?

3. What part of the world did it live in?

4. What protective features does it have?

5. What type of food did it eat?

6. How many vertebrae does it have?

7. How many toes does it have?

8. Are the front and back feet the same?

9. If not, how are they different?

10. Which part of the body has the largest circumference?

Write a story in your log book about one or more dinosaurs in the exhibit. Here are some suggested topics:

- If I Had a Dinosaur for a Pet
- If Dinosaurs Lived Today
- If I Lived During the Age of the Dinosaurs
- If Dinosaurs Could Talk

Natural History Museum Visit: Habitat Scene

Objective: To become familiar with a habitat scene in a natural history museum.

Materials

Camera or drawing materials

Log book

Pencil

Procedure

Select one of the museum's dioramas or habitat scenes to study. Dioramas and habitat scenes are scenes made up of stuffed animals placed in what looks like a natural setting.

Take photographs, draw pictures, or buy postcards of the scene.

Study the scene carefully to answer the following questions about it. (You may also want to refer to museum pamphlets or talk to a museum guide.) Record the answers in your log book.

1. What is the name of the scene (or its subject, if it doesn't have a name)?
2. How many animals are in the scene?
3. How many different kinds of animals are in the scene?
4. Are there any animals with feathers in the scene? If so, name them.
5. What things are in the scene in addition to animals?
6. Are there any animals with manes? If so, name them.
7. Which animal is the tallest?
8. Which animals are shorter than you are?
9. Which animals do you think are the best runners? Why?
10. What time of day does the scene depict? What clues does the scene give you about what time of day it is?
11. What do the animals in the scene have in common?
12. Are any animals looking at you? Which ones? Why?
13. Which animal do you think eats the most?
14. Which animal do you think weighs the most?
15. If this scene were real, what odors would you smell?
16. If this scene were real, what do you think would happen next?
17. What would be good background music for this scene?
18. Would you like to pet any of these animals? Which ones? Why?
19. If you could be any one of these animals, which would you be? Why?
20. What would you be thinking and feeling if you were sitting in a tree above the animals?
21. Do you think you would like to visit this place? Why or why not?
22. In one word, how would you describe your feelings about this scene?

Natural History Museum Visit: Indians

Objective: To become familiar with the Indian exhibit in a natural history museum.

Materials

Camera or drawing materials

Log book

Pencil

Procedure

Visit the museum's Indian exhibit.

Take photographs, draw pictures, or buy postcards of the exhibit.

Study the exhibit carefully to obtain the following information about it. (You may also want to refer to museum pamphlets or talk to a museum guide.) Record the information in your log book.

1. Estimate the sizes (length and width, or diameter and depth) of a peace pipe, a bow, an arrow, and a few baskets.

2. Find items that are used in sets, and note the number used in each set. (For example, snowshoes are used in a set of two.)

3. (Optional) Estimate the dimensions of a snowshoe if there is one in the exhibit.

4. Find some geometric shapes in the display. Draw them in your log book, and note what they are or where they are used.

5. Count the number of claws used in a collar or necklace, and determine the number of animal paws used to make it.

6. Estimate the area of floor space in a tepee or other Indian dwelling, and calculate the amount of space per person if four people lived in the dwelling.

7. (Optional) If there is more than one tepee in the exhibit, count the number of poles used to construct each tepee. Is the number of poles the same for each one?

8. Study the foods the Indians eat. What food is eaten the most?

9. What animals do the Indians hunt? How is each part of the animal used?

10. Describe one of the scenes in the exhibit. Would you like to be a part of this scene? Why or why not?

Natural History Museum Visit: Mummies

Objective: To become familiar with the ancient Egypt exhibit in a natural history museum.

Materials

 Camera or drawing materials

 Log book

 Pencil

Procedure

Visit the museum's ancient Egypt exhibit.

 Take photographs, draw pictures, or buy postcards of the mummies and other interesting items in the exhibit.

Imagine that you are one of the mummies when he or she was alive. Study the exhibit and answer the following questions in your log book.

1. What do you wear on your head?
2. What do you wear on your feet?
3. What do you wear on your body?
4. Is this apparel comfortable? Why or why not?
5. What utensils do you use for eating and for cooking?
6. What other items in the exhibit would you use for everyday living? How would they be used?
7. When were you born? How long did you live?

Now answer the following questions about the exhibit.

8. (Optional) If there is more than one mummy in the exhibit, describe five ways in which two of them are alike and five ways in which they are different.
9. Are ancient Egyptian burial practices similar in any way to those of today?
10. What evidence can be found in the exhibits that reflects the ancient Egyptians' belief in an afterlife?
11. What question would you most like to ask one of the mummies?

In your log book, write a story about one of the mummies when he or she was alive.

Painted Leaf Prints

Objectives: To make prints of leaves from the vacation site.
   To identify the leaves collected.

Materials

   Leaves
   Tempera paints
   White paper
   Newspapers
   Small paintbrush
   Tree identification book
   Log book
   Pencil

Method 1

Method 2

Procedure

Collect several different kinds of leaves from your vacation area.

   Use the tree identification book to identify the leaves you have collected.

✎ Record the names of the plants in your log book.

   Make prints of the leaves, using one of the two following methods.

   Method 1: Apply tempera paint to the bottom of the leaf. Put the leaf bottom up on a flat surface (protected with newspaper). Place a piece of white paper over the leaf, and press down firmly and evenly over the leaf until the paint is dry. (You might make an interesting picture with several leaves arranged in a pattern.)

   Method 2: Place the leaf on the sheet of white paper, and spatter paint over it. Carefully, lift the leaf off the paper when you are done spattering the paint.

   Print the name of each leaf under its picture.

✎ In your log book, write a story or a poem about your leaf prints.

Park, Forest Preserve, or Nature Center Visit

Objective: To observe and compare animals and plants.

Materials

    Camera or drawing material
    Plant and animal identification
        books
    Sun print paper (optional)
    Log book
    Pencil

Procedure

First, just walk around and look. Take in the whole picture. Then describe in your log book what you see.

Now, select some animals and plants to identify more specifically, using your identification books. Use your own method to record information in your log book about the plants and animals, or use the following formats.

For animals: 1. Animal name
                 2. Description of animal
                 3. Description of animal's behavior
                 4. Photograph or drawing of the animal
                 5. Detail of the animal, such as a feather or a drawing of a footprint

For plants: 1. Plant name
                 2. Description of plant
                 3. Description of plant's location (such as shady or sunny, cool or warm, moist or dry)
                 4. Photograph or drawing (or sun print) of the plant

Select two plants to compare and contrast. Enter the comparison in your log book. For example, a comparison of a maple tree and an oak tree might begin like this:

Comparison of a Maple Tree and an Oak Tree

SIMILARITIES	DIFFERENCES
green	shape of leaf

Select two animals to compare and contrast. Enter the comparison in your log book. Use the same format as that for plants.

Planetarium Visit

Objective: To visit a planetarium and learn about planets, stars, and the universe.

Materials
> Drawing materials
> Log book
> Pencil

Procedure

As you tour the planetarium, find the following information. Record it in your log book.

1. Name of the planetarium
2. City in which it is located
3. Special features of the planetarium

PLANETS

4. Make a data table of the planets in order of their distance from the sun. Start with the planet closest to the sun. The columns in the table should show the planet's name, the planet's size, the number of its moons, its distance from the sun, and one interesting fact about the planet. Your table might have these column names:

PLANET	DIAMETER (MILES)	MOONS	DISTANCE FROM SUN (MILLION MILES)	INTERESTING FACT

GALAXIES

5. Name the different types of galaxies.
6. In which galaxy is our solar system found?
7. What is the closest galaxy to the one our planet is found in? How far away is it?
8. Name some other interesting galaxies.

CONSTELLATIONS

9. Name five constellations and tell where they are located in the sky.
10. Tell how each of these five constellations was given its name.

TELESCOPES

11. List the different types of telescopes. Briefly explain how each one works.
12. Who invented the different types of telescopes?
13. Where is the largest reflecting telescope located?
14. Where is the largest refracting telescope located?

> *Extra Credit:* What is the Hubble Space Telescope?

The Playground: Swing Science

Objective: To use playground swings to study the motion of a pendulum.

Materials

    Stopwatch or watch with a second hand
    Log book
    Pencil

Procedure

You will need two people to help you with this experiment.

- Get on the shortest swing.

- Have one of your helpers pull you back to his or her shoulder height and release you. Just swing—do not pump.

- Have the other helper time you for one minute.

Count the number of swings you make in one minute, and record it in a data table in your log book. Do two more one-minute trials, and calculate the average number of swings. The data table should be set up something like this:

TRIAL	SHORT SWING No. of swings	LONG SWING No. of swings
1		
2		
3		
Average		

- Now go to the longest swing and repeat the above process.

Have your helpers repeat the same experiment. Record this information in a data table in your log book.

Now, compare the data tables for each person who experimented with the swings and write the answers to the following questions in your log book.

    1. What variables did you use?
    2. What conditions are best for the greatest number of swings?

Rock Classification I

Objective: To collect and group rocks by color.

Materials

Box for collecting
Boxes or bags for grouping
Log book
Pencil

Procedure

Collect a variety of small rocks from the area you are visiting. Sort the rocks by color.

In your log book,

1. describe each group of rocks, and

2. tell if there is another way to group the rocks.

Rock Classification II

Objective: To collect, identify, and classify rocks that are native to the vacation site.

Materials

    Collecting bags
    Rock identification book
    White-out
    Black felt-tip pen
    Clear nail polish
    Super glue
    Display box (see "How to Make a Display Box,"
      page 27)
    Log book
    Pencil

Procedure

- Collect a variety of small rocks from the area you are visiting.

- Use the rock identification book to determine the types of rocks you have collected.

- Number each rock by putting a small spot of white-out on it and writing the number on the spot with the black pen. Coat the number with clear nail polish.

 In your log book, make a list of the rocks by number. Write the names of the rocks next to the numbers.

- When you get back from your vacation, make a display box.

- Make an index card with the name and number of each rock and information about it.

- Glue the rocks into the display box.

- Put the index cards in the small box in the display box.

Science Museum Visit

Objective: To become aware of and to analyze exhibits in a science museum.

Materials

    Camera or drawing materials
    Log book
    Pencil

Procedure
Select two exhibits in the museum to research. The exhibits should be quite different from each other.

Take photographs, draw pictures, or buy postcards or slides of the exhibits.

For each exhibit, find out the answers to the following questions. Record the answers in your log book.

1. What is the name of the museum and the title of the exhibit?
2. What is the name of the gallery, hall, or area in which it is located?
3. What is the purpose of the exhibit?
4. What is the size of the exhibit?
5. What objects are included in the exhibit?
6. How are the objects arranged in the exhibit?
7. What colors appear in the exhibit?
8. What kind of lighting is used (such as direct, indirect, spotlights)?
9. Is the exhibit by itself, or is it part of a larger exhibit?
10. If it is part of a larger exhibit, how does it relate to the larger exhibit?
11. Is it easy to get through the exhibit area? Why or why not?
12. How many people can view this exhibit at one time? (Consider sight lines, arrangement of objects, and position and number of labels.)
13. What is the first thing you notice in the exhibit? Why?
14. What is the most interesting part of the exhibit to you? Why?
15. What are you supposed to do at the exhibit?
16. What is the main message or theme of the exhibit?
17. How do you feel about the design of the exhibit?
18. What else would you like to see in the exhibit to help you understand it better?

Use the pictures and the information in your log book to prepare a presentation to the class about your visit to the science museum.

(Optional) Many science museums have hands-on demonstrations. Do one of these demonstrations, and describe it in your log book. When you return to school, be prepared to explain the demonstration to the class. If the necessary supplies are available, you can repeat the demonstration for the class.

Sea Life Park Visit

Objective: To become familiar with the animal life in a sea life park.

Materials

Camera or drawing materials
Log book
Pencil

Procedure

Take photographs, draw pictures, or buy postcards or slides of each animal you visit.

Find out the following information about each animal you see, and write the information in your log book.

1. Type of animal

2. Animal's name

3. Age of the animal

4. Trainer's name

5. What the animal eats

6. How fast the animal can swim

7. Where the animal lived before it came to the park

8. How the animal was trained

9. (Optional) If you can touch the animal, how it feels

Use the information and the pictures to prepare an oral report to present to the class after you return from vacation.

It is often possible to go behind the scenes at sea life parks. If you are able to do this, write a paragraph in your log book about your visit behind the scenes.
If such a visit is not possible, write a paragraph, a story, or a poem in your log book about the animal or activity you enjoyed the most.

Make a poster about your favorite animal or animals at the park.

Seed Pictures

Objective: To make pictures using the seeds found in the vacation area.

Materials

A variety of different seeds

Bags for collecting each kind of seed

Plant identification book

Poster board or cardboard, about 8" x 10"

Strong glue

Log book

Pencil

Procedure

- Collect a variety of seeds. Note the kinds of plants they come from, and identify the plants in the identification book.

- Draw a picture on the poster board. Do not make it too difficult or elaborate.

- With the glue, draw over the outside lines and other important lines in the picture.

- Put the largest seeds on the important lines.

- Decide where your other seeds would look best.

- Spread glue over the section where you want a certain kind of seed, and put the **seeds** on the glue.

- When you have finished placing all your seeds, set the picture aside to dry.

- When the picture is dry, check to see that all the seeds are still in place. Reglue those that have come loose.

In your log book,

1. draw a smaller version of your seed picture, and on it,

2. label the types of seeds used on the various parts of your picture.

Shadow Pictures

Objective: To draw pictures of objects from their shadows.

Materials

    Drawing paper
    Pencil
    Lamp (or bright sunlight)
    Magazine or clipboard

Procedure

- Select an object to draw—such as a leaf or a small plant.

- If necessary, secure the object so that it is standing upright.

- Use the lamp or position the object in bright sunlight so that you get a sharp shadow.

- Place a piece of paper (clipped to a clipboard or magazine) where the shadow falls. The magazine or clipboard under the paper will ensure a firm, level surface on which to draw.

- Draw around the shadow. Color in the picture, if you like.

- If possible, make a shadow picture of the object at different times of the day. Record the time of day when each picture is made. Explain why the shadow changes.

In your log book, write a descriptive paragraph about your picture.

Shell Collection I

Objective: To collect, identify, and classify shells.

Materials

Collection bags

Shell identification book

Cardboard sheet or box for displaying shells

Glue

Pencil

Procedure

- Visit the beach and collect a variety of shells.

- Sort the shells. Classify the shells by size or color.

- Glue the shells to the cardboard or the box.

- Find the shells in the shell identification book, and prepare a small card with information about each shell. Place the card below the shell or in a small box next to the display.

Shell Collection II

Objective: To collect, identify, and classify shells.

Materials

Collection bags

Shell identification book

Cardboard sheet or box for displaying shells

Glue

Pencil

Procedure

- Visit the beach and collect a variety of shells.

- Sort the shells. Use the identification book and classify the shells by type.

- Glue the shells to the cardboard or the box.

- Prepare a small card with information about each shell. Place the card below the shell or in a small box next to the display.

Skiing: Pulse Rate

Objective: To observe the effect of skiing on the pulse rate.

Materials
    Stopwatch or watch with a second hand
    Log book
    Pencil

Procedure
Take your pulse while you are resting, and record it in the log book. To find your pulse rate per minute, count the number of beats for 15 seconds and multiply that number by four.

Check your pulse rate again while you are waiting to ski. Remember it so that you can record it later in your log book.

Take your pulse once more right after the ski run. Remember it so that you can record it later in your log book.

Repeat this process for a number of ski runs. If you ski on different slopes, record their location, too.

After you finish skiing, add the following to your log book.

1. Prepare a data table with your information. Your table should be set up similar to the one below.

Pulse Rates Before and After Skiing

TIME OF SKI RUN	PULSE RATE	
	WAITING	AFTER

Extra Credit: Prepare a line graph comparing pulse rates for each trip down the slopes.

---

2. Describe your feelings while waiting to ski and while skiing. If you skiied on different slopes, did you feel differently about skiing down any of them? If so, what were the different feelings? What might have caused them?
3. On which run was your pulse rate the highest? Explain what might have caused this.

In your log book, write a story about your ski trip.

Snowdrift Adventure

Objectives: To see the layers in a snowdrift.
To compare the temperatures of the different levels of a snowdrift.

Materials

Thermometer (with both Celsius and
    Fahrenheit scales)

Hand lens

Shovel

Graph paper

Ruler

Log book

Pen or pencil

Procedure

Find a really neat big snowdrift (a little one will do if you can't find a big one).

With the shovel, dig down into the snowdrift as straight as you can so that you can see the levels.

Measure the thickness of each level. Describe the color of each level. Take the temperature of each level in Celsius and Fahrenheit. (Be sure to wait until the thermometer liquid has stopped rising or falling before you record the temperature.) Record these three kinds of information in your log book in a data table set up something like this:

LEVEL	THICKNESS	COLOR	TEMPERATURE
1			
2			
3			

Look at the snow at each level with the hand lens. In your log book, describe what you see.

On the graph paper, prepare a line graph of the temperature readings at the different levels. Attach this graph to a blank page in your log book.

Answer the following questions in your log book.

1. Which level of the snowdrift is the coldest?
2. Is the snow or the air colder?
3. Which layer of snow is the thickest? Why do you think it is the thickest?

Snowflake Observation

Objectives: To observe snowflakes and classify them according to the International Classification of Snow Crystals.

To make a paper replica of a snowflake.

Materials

Snow

Paper

Hand lens

"International Classification of Snow Crystals" chart (page 77)

Drawing compass or round object

Glue

Protractor

Log book

Pencil

Procedure

Go outside during or just after a snowfall. Catch snowflakes on your clothing. Observe the flakes with the hand lens.

In your log book, draw pictures of the snowflakes. Compare the pictures. Look at the "International Classification of Snow Crystals" chart, and label each snowflake picture according to its classification in the chart.

On a separate page in your log book, make a bar graph of your snowflakes, using the classifications on the chart as headings.

Make a snowflake that looks like one you observed (see "How to Make a Paper Snowflake," page 76).

HOW TO MAKE A PAPER SNOWFLAKE

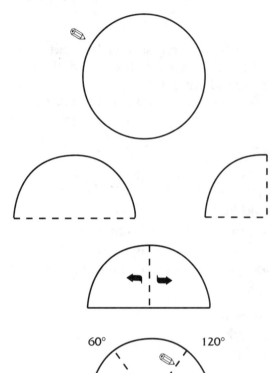

- Use the compass (or round object) to draw a circle the size you want. Cut out the circle.

- Fold the circle in half. Then fold the half circle in half.

- Unfold the quarter circle back into a half circle.

60°   120°

- Use the protractor to mark 60° and 120° on the half circle. Draw lines along these marks from the midline point to the edge.

- Fold along these lines so that the half circle is now in thirds.

- Fold again down the center line.

- Draw a pattern along the thick fold. DO NOT CUT OFF THE POINT. Cut carefully along the lines you have drawn.

- Carefully unfold the paper and observe your snowflake.

- Glue your snowflake into your log book. Or make more snowflakes, and mount them on a poster board for a classroom display. Label the different types of snowflakes on your poster.

  Go and Have a Good Time © 1990 Fearon Teacher Aids

INTERNATIONAL CLASSIFICATION OF SNOW CRYSTALS

SYMBOL	NAME OF CRYSTAL	EXAMPLES
	Capped Columns	
	Irregular Crystals	
	Graupel (soft hail)	
	Sleet	
	Hail	
	Hexagonal Plates	
	Stellar Crystals	
	Hexagonal Columns	
	Needles	
	Spatial Dendrites	

Space Center Visit

Objective: To gain information about space travel.

Materials
> Camera
> Log book
> Pencil

Procedure

As you tour the space center, look for the following information and record it in your log book.

1. List five types of space satellites and tell how each is used.

2. List five space projects and briefly explain the goal of each one.

3. Describe an experiment that was performed on the space shuttle. Briefly explain its purpose, and, if possible, describe its results.

4. Look for moon rocks on display. Tell some facts about them. How did they get to earth? How old are they? What materials are found in them?

5. Look at a spacesuit. Look at what you are wearing today. List three differences between the spacesuit and your clothing.

6. Make a time line of the space program.

7. Take photographs of rockets or spacecraft on display. Put the pictures in your log book and label them.

Write a paragraph to describe your visit. Include in your paragraph one piece of interesting information that is not included in the information above.
    Or write a fictional story describing your adventures as a member of a space shuttle crew, a Skylab crew, or a moon-landing crew.

Stargazing

Objective: To observe constellations, planets, and the moon.

Materials

Star map or chart
"How to Locate Stars" sheet
  (page 80)
Compass
Binoculars
Telescope (if available)
Drawing materials
Log book
Pencil

Procedure

Go outside on a clear night in an area as far away from city lights as possible. Before you go, read the sheet "How to Locate Stars."

Use the star map or chart to locate as many constellations as possible. Record the following information about each one in your log book:

1. where each constellation appears in the sky,
2. how high it is above the horizon, and
3. any other interesting facts about the constellation.

Record the names of any planets you see. Write down the time you see each one and its location in the sky.

Observe the moon. At what phase is it? Record this information in your log book.

Look at the moon with binoculars, and describe in your log book what you see. Compare how the moon looks through binoculars to how it looks to the unaided eye.

Draw a picture of the moon each night of your trip. Label the type of moon you see each night—full, waxing, waning, quarter, or new.

(Optional) Observe the planets, the moon, and the stars with the telescope. Describe or draw a picture in your log book of what you see. How does the view through the telescope compare with the view through binoculars and with what the unaided eye sees?

HOW TO LOCATE STARS

First, make sure that your star map is turned to the correct time of the correct day and month—and that it's pointing in the same direction that you are facing. (Use a compass to be sure.)

Then you need to know how to relate what you see on the star map to what you see in the sky. The locations of stars in the sky are measured in degrees—just like the locations of places on the globe are identified by degrees of longitude and latitude. There are celestial poles and a celestial equator in the sky, just like there are poles and an equator on the earth.

From the horizon to the zenith (the point directly overhead) is 90°. And on the sky map, it is 90° from the edge of the circle to the center point. In other words, the stars at the edge of the circle on the sky map are the ones you see just above the horizon, and the stars in the center of the sky map are the ones you see directly overhead.

But how do you identify what's in between? Here's a simple way to estimate degrees of distance in space. Make a fist and hold it at arm's length. Sight past your fist with one eye. Your fist covers about 10° of sky from thumb to little finger.

An outstretched hand covers about 20° of sky from thumbtip to little fingertip.

A fingernail at arm's length is about 1° wide.

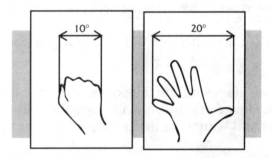

You can estimate a constellation's distance in degrees above the horizon by measuring how many hands high it is. Hold your hand outstretched and sideways with your thumb at the horizon. Look carefully at where the tip of your little finger is, and move your thumb there. Continue moving your hand up the sky like this until you've reached the constellation. Multiply the number of hands between the horizon and the constellation by 20° for the approximate location of the constellation.

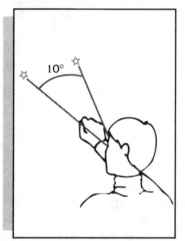

Of course, hands aren't all the same size. If you want to be more precise about how many degrees your hand actually covers, test it on the Big Dipper. The stars on the bottom of the dipper bowl are 8° apart. The distance from the left-hand star at the bottom of the bowl to the star at the start of the handle is 4.5°. The distance between the stars on the top of the bowl is 10°. The distance between the star at the top right and the star at the bottom right of the bowl is 5°. These two stars are the pointer stars that point to the North Star, or Polaris, which is 30° away.

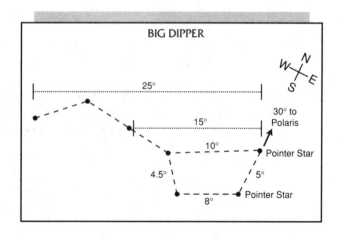

Sun Prints

Objective: To become aware of the plants in a particular area.

Materials

- Sun print paper (available in hobby shops)
- Leaves or other small objects
- Small stones or Plexiglas sheet
- Small board, tray, or clipboard
- Water
- Paper towels
- Shallow pan
- Newspaper
- Plant identification book
- Log book
- Pencil

Procedure

A sunny day is the best time to do this activity. Keep the sun print paper out of the light until you are ready to use it.

- Select leaves from various trees and plants. (You can also make sun prints of any other small objects you find in the area.) Use the plant identification book to identify the leaves you've selected.

- Put the paper on a board, tray, or clipboard so that you can carry it easily. Arrange the objects on the blue side of the sun paper. Weigh them down with the stones or the Plexiglas sheet if the day is windy. (Be sure that the stones do not go over the edges of the objects; if any do, you'll get the silhouette of part of the stone as well as of the object.)

- Carefully place the paper with the objects on it in the sun. (You can make sun prints on a cloudy day, but they will take longer to develop. Developing will also take longer if you use a Plexiglas sheet as the weight.)

- Leave the paper in the sun until the paper becomes light.

- Carefully carry the paper on the board, tray, or clipboard (with the objects still on it) inside or to a shady area where the shallow pan of water is waiting.

- When you are next to the pan of water, remove the objects from the paper. Place the paper in the water.

- While the print is developing, get the newspaper and place it beside the pan.

- When the silhouette becomes dark blue and the unexposed area becomes white, the print is ready to take out of the water.

● Place the picture with the printed side up on the newspaper, and allow it to air dry. Blot excess water with the paper towels.

✏️ When the picture is dry, put it in your log book, and label the page with the name of each plant and its location and habitat. Here's an example of a page format.

Location: Northern Illinois

Habitat: Forest

place sun print here

Plants: Black Oak, White Oak, Hickory

(Optional) Make a poster of sun prints of leaves collected from several places. Identify the location, habitat, and names of the plants following the example above. Display the poster in your classroom.

Tidepools

Objective: To observe tidepools and the seashore.

Materials

Seashore life identification book

Wooden stick (such as chopstick or popsicle stick—*not metal*)

Drawing materials

Log book

Pencil

Procedure

Go to a rocky beach and find a tidepool.

Sit facing the water, and observe the tidepool without touching anything. Write a description in your log book and draw a picture of what you observe.

Next, carefully turn over some rocks. Observe what is under them. Use the seashore life identification book to identify any animals you see. Write a description in your log book and draw a picture of what you observe. Put the rocks back in place so that the small creatures that live under them can return to their homes.

Now probe in the water and the sand of the tidepool with your wooden stick. Write a description in your log book and draw a picture of any new creatures you see.

(Optional) Return to the same tidepool one or more times during your visit. Try to observe the tidepool at various times of day. Compare and contrast these visits. How was the tidepool the same, and how was it different? Does the time of day during your visit make a difference?

Trees

Objective: To become more aware of the trees in the area visited.

Materials

- Tree identification book
- Yardstick or meter stick
- Dark-color crayons with paper removed
- Bond or butcher paper
- Waxed paper
- Cellophane tape
- Log book
- Pencil

Procedure

✏ In your log book, describe the area you are visiting. Are there many trees, a moderate number, or only a few? Is the area an old woods, a young woods, or some type of orchard?

Use the tree identification book to identify four or more types of trees. If you are visiting an orchard, see if there are different varieties of fruit trees.

✏ Collect a variety of leaves. Identify them. Press them. Then place them in your log book. To keep them in place, cover the page with waxed paper and secure the paper with cellophane tape.

Select one tree to "adopt."

Estimate the height of your adopted tree. To do this: (1) place a yardstick or meter stick perpendicular to the ground and measure the length of its shadow, (2) measure the length of the tree's shadow, and then (3) use those figures to solve this proportion:

$$\frac{\text{Shadow of tree}}{\text{Shadow of stick}} = \frac{\text{Tree's height}}{\text{Stick's height}}$$

For example, if a yardstick (3 feet long) casts a shadow that is 2 feet long, and the tree casts a shadow that is 10 feet long, how high is the tree? The proportion would be

$$\frac{10}{2} = \frac{\text{Tree's height}}{3}$$

Therefore, the tree's height would be 15 feet.

✏ Record the estimate of your tree's height in your log book.

Do a rubbing of your adopted tree's bark by placing the bond or butcher paper on the bark and rubbing the side of the paper with the crayon. You can also make a rubbing of a leaf or leaves, using this same technique.

✏ In your log book, write a story or a poem about your tree, or about the entire area.

✏ (Optional) If you can find a stump or log of a tree that has been cut down, count the rings to determine the age of the tree when it was cut. (One ring equals one year.) You can also determine rainfall patterns by looking at the rings. If they are close together, there was little rain. If they are far apart, there was a lot of rain. Record the information you can observe from the tree rings in your log book.

Washington, D.C., Visit

Objective: To gain information about buildings and monuments in Washington, D.C.

Materials

    Camera
    Log book
    Pencil

Procedure

✏️ While you are touring Washington, D.C., take pictures of the monuments and buildings you visit. Try to find out the answers to the following questions about them, and record the answers in your log book.

1. Why is the Executive Mansion called the White House? (Yes, it is painted white, but why?)

2. What figure, surrounded by Italian green marble, is in the center of the rotunda of the Capitol Building? Of what kind of metal is it made?

3. Why does the Washington Monument have two colors of stone?

4. How tall is the Washington Monument?

5. What famous new memorial is across from the Lincoln Memorial?

6. Is Lincoln's body buried in the Lincoln Memorial?

7. What quotations are inscribed on the Lincoln Memorial?

8. What saying is printed at the Jefferson Memorial?

9. What type of material was used to build the Jefferson Memorial?

10. What famous monument has these words inscribed on it: "Here rests in honored glory an American soldier, known but to God"?

✏️ Washington, D.C., has many other outstanding features. Select your favorite and write about it.

Weather Comparison

Objective: To compare the weather of the vacation site to the weather at home.

Materials

Weather reports from vacation site

Weather reports from home

Glue

Log book

Pencil

Procedure

Ask a friend or neighbor to save newspapers from home while you are away or to write down the radio or TV weather reports.

Refer to the newspaper at your vacation site for daily weather forecasts. Keep a daily weather record in your log book. Be sure to include

1. the high and low temperatures,
2. the barometer reading,
3. the wind speed,
4. the wind direction,
5. the cloud cover,
6. the amount and type of precipitation, and
7. the type and position of fronts.

After your vacation, make a graph or data table comparing the weather at home and at your vacation site. For added interest, you might glue the weather maps from each day in your log book.

Go and Have a Good Time © 1990 Fearon Teacher Aids

Wild Flowers

Objective: To become aware of the flowers at the vacation site.

Materials

    Wild flower identification book
    Camera or drawing materials
    Log book
    Pencil

Procedure

Go for a walk and observe the flowers. Be sure to take time to smell the flowers along the way. But don't pick any unless you have permission.

Use the wild flower identification book to try to identify the flowers you see.

In your log book, write a description of each type of flower. Make a drawing or take a photograph of each kind of flower. If you are allowed to pick the flowers, you could press them.

Prepare a presentation for the class about the wild flowers you have seen.

(Optional) If you see a large field of flowers, estimate how many of each type are in the field. Record your estimate in your log book.

If you can count the number, make a bar graph in your log book of the types of flowers (classify them by color or by another method of your choice) and the number of each type.

Wild Foods

Objective: To obtain edible wild foods and prepare them for family and friends while on vacation.

Materials

Cooking equipment
Collecting equipment
Wild food guide*
"Wild Food Recipes" sheet (page 89)
Other ingredients as necessary
Drawing materials or camera
Poster board
Log book
Pencil

Procedure

This is a good activity for adventuresome campers and lovers of the outdoors.

- Use the wild food identification book and explore an area for edible wild foods. Be aware of poisonous plants (and of poisonous parts of edible plants), and do not collect plants from roadsides, because of pollution.
- Some common edible plants are day lilies, cattails, purple violets, dandelions, pumpkin blossoms, red clover, berries, and spearmint.
- Take photographs or draw pictures of the area and of the plants you collect.
- After you have collected the wild foods, follow the recipes on the "Wild Food Recipes" sheet (or other recipes you may find) to prepare a meal for your family.

✏️ Ask each person who tastes your dishes to make a comment in your log book about them.

- Make a poster for classroom display of the wild foods you collected. If possible, bring some of the foods to share with the class.

---

* Two good wild food guides are *Tom Brown's Guide to Wild Edible and Medicinal Plants* by Tom Brown, Jr. (Berkley Books, 1985) and *Your Own Food: A Forager's Guide* by Dan Jason (Intermedia, 1979).

WILD FOOD RECIPES

CLOVER PANCAKES

Collect and wash ½ cup of red clover, and add it to the batter of your favorite pancake recipe. Prepare pancakes as usual.

APPLE-SPEARMINT SALAD

Collect and wash 1 cup of wild spearmint, and add it to your favorite apple salad recipe.

SPEARMINT TEA

Collect 1 cup of spearmint leaves. Boil 4 cups of water, and add leaves to the water. Let steep for about 10 minutes. Add sugar to taste. Serve hot, or add ice and serve.

DAY LILY FRITTERS

Collect day lily blossoms. Wash them and remove the centers. Prepare your favorite pancake batter, and add about ½ cup more milk to make the batter thinner. Dip the blossoms in the batter. Deep fry them. Remove the blossoms, and drain them on paper towels. Dip in powdered sugar.

This recipe can also be used with pumpkin blossoms.

For a simpler dish, dip the blossoms in beaten eggs and fry them in a skillet with a little vegetable oil.

Write a Poem

Objective: To describe a favorite part of your vacation in a short poem.

Materials

    Log book

    Pencil

Procedure

Select a favorite animal, object, or scene from your vacation, and, in your log book, write a cinquain or a haiku about it. Cinquains and haikus are short, rhymeless forms of poems.

A cinquain is a five-line poem. The first line is one word, which is the subject of the poem. The second line is two words describing the subject of the poem. The third line is three words depicting the subject's actions. The fourth line is four words that convey feeling. And the fifth line is one word that refers to the first line. Here is an example of a cinquain.

Dinosaur

Prehistoric giant

Lumbering, roaring, quaking

Fascinating, fearsome, amazing, awesome

Reptile

          —J. Townsend

A haiku is usually about nature and consists of three lines. The first and third lines each have five syllables. The second line has seven syllables. Here are two examples of haikus.

Bright and colorful sky

Buzzing, humming, soaring flight

Butterflies, bees, moths

          —R. West

Quiet desert night

Lowing, calling, cattle sounds

Tepees, chiefs, and braves

          —R. West

Zoo Excursion: Birds

Objective: To observe and record facts about birds in the zoo.

Materials

    Camera or drawing materials
    Log book
    Pencil

Procedure

✏️ Read the information below, and then look for examples of birds with the various kinds of beaks and feet as you tour the zoo. Record the information in your log book. Take photographs or draw pictures of your favorite birds.

TYPES OF BEAKS

Birds do not have teeth; they use their beaks to get mouthfuls of food. The shapes of their beaks are adapted to the kind of food they eat. Look at the following illustrations of types of beaks.

Find two kinds of birds with each type of beak. Give their names, and tell what kind of food they eat.

FISH-EATING BEAK
The fish-eating beak is long, slim, and strong. It is pointed so that the bird can reach into the water and grasp slippery creatures.

INSECT-CATCHING BEAK
The insect-catching beak, also known as the trap bill, is small and can open wide so that the bird, while flying, can grab insects.

INSECT- AND FRUIT-EATING BEAK

The insect- and fruit-eating beak is narrow and pointed so that the bird can grab insects or reach fruits. It is slightly arched so that the bird can crack seeds. This kind of beak is longer than an insect-catching beak but shorter than a fish-eating beak, and it is sleeker and longer than a seed-eating beak.

SEED-EATING BEAK

The seed-eating beak is arched into the shape of a cone. It is stout and sharp so that the bird can crack seeds.

WATER- AND MUD-SIFTING BEAK

The water- and mud-sifting beak is wide and shallow. It has comblike strainers on the edges to filter bits of food out of the water.

CHISEL BEAK

The chisel beak is sturdy and sharply pointed so that the bird can chisel into wood. It is accompanied by an extremely long barb-tipped tongue to pull insects and insect eggs out of tunnels in bark or wood.

PREYING BEAK

The preying beak is stout, sharp, and sharply hooked so that the bird can tear the flesh of animals.

PROBING BEAK

The probing beak is thin and long so that the bird can reach insects and other small animals buried in mud or sand. A nectar-eating beak is similar and is accompanied by a tongue whose sides curl to form a double trough to carry the nectar.

TYPES OF FEET

The shape of birds' feet is adapted to where the birds live and what they eat. Look at the following illustrations of types of feet.

Find one type of bird with each type of foot. Name the bird, describe the area it lives in, and explain how the shape of its feet help it survive.

PREYING FEET

Preying, or grasping, feet are used for seizing and carrying live prey. They have sharp, curved claws, or talons. These are used to catch, crush, and carry away prey.

PERCHING FEET

Perching feet are used to hold onto branches to keep the bird from falling. There are three toes in the front and one in the back.

CLIMBING FEET

Climbing feet are used to help the bird climb and clutch the bark of a tree. The feet have sharp, curved claws with two toes pointed forward and two pointed backward. These back toes act as a brace.

WADING FEET

Wading feet help the bird wade in ponds and streams, where it catches and eats small water animals. Some waders have only three toes, which point forward. Others also have a small hind toe.

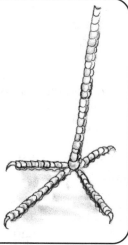

SWIMMING FEET: WEBBED VERSION

Webbed swimming feet are used to paddle through the water. There are three toes with webs between them, and there is a small toe in the back.

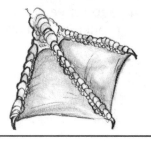

SWIMMING FEET: LOBED VERSION

Lobed swimming feet are also used to paddle through the water. Each toe on this type of foot is like a tiny paddle.

Zoo Excursion: Mammals and Reptiles

Objective: To observe and record facts about zoo mammals and reptiles

Materials

    Camera or drawing materials

    Log book

    Pencil

Procedure

Before you go to the zoo, decide with your teacher which animal groups you will study.

✏️ Look through the questions for each animal group you are going to study, and then find the answers as you tour the zoo. Record the information in your log book.

CAMELS

Camels live in desert regions. Deserts are usually hot and dry during the day and cold at night.

1. Look at the camel's coat. Notice how fine and woolly it is around the hump. Where on the hump is the fur the thickest? How would the thick fur on this part of the hump help the camel to survive in the daytime? What is the purpose of the hump?

2. Compare the size of the camel's foot to the size of a giraffe's foot. Which animal has the larger foot? Suggest a reason for this.

3. There is often sand and dust in the desert. What does the camel have to protect its eyes from sand and dust?

CHIMPANZEES, MONKEYS, AND APES

1. Mammals often spend more time caring for their young and for each other than other vertebrates do. Record the ways you see chimpanzees, monkeys, and apes caring for their young and for each other.

2. Compare the behaviors of young chimpanzees, monkeys, and apes.

GIRAFFES

Giraffes live in open grasslands in Central and Southern Africa. They eat leaves, shoots, and the bark of acacia trees. Their only competitors for food are elephants. Their main predators are lions.

1. What is the main color of the giraffe?
2. What is the advantage of the broken color pattern on its body?
3. In what way is the giraffe's height an advantage?
4. Look at the giraffe's head. How many "horns" does it have?
5. Watch the giraffe eat. Describe how it uses its tongue and lips.
6. How does the giraffe escape from predators?
7. Compare the giraffe's foot with a horse's foot. How do they differ?

REPTILES

1. A reptile is coldblooded. What does this mean?
2. What is the largest reptile in the zoo? What is its native habitat? What does it eat? Estimate its size.
3. What is one difference between snakes and lizards?
4. Describe the type of skin that covers the reptiles.

SEALS AND SEA LIONS

1. List the features you can see showing that seals and sea lions are mammals.
2. Describe or draw their body shape.
3. What happens to their nostrils when they dive under water?
4. Time how long one of the seals can stay under water. Repeat this measurement four times. Find the average length of time a seal can stay under water.